Human
ACTIVATION
GUIDE

Introduction to Your
QUANTUM BLUEPRINT

Karen Curry Parker

GracePoint Matrix, LLC
Publishing Division

Human Design Activation Guide:
Introduction to Your Quantum Blueprint

ISBN: 978-0-9976035-4-5 paperback – black and white
978-0-9976035-6-9 paperback - color
978-0-9976035-5-2 eBook

Published by
GracePoint Matrix, Publishing Division
322 N. Tejon St. Suite 208
Colorado Springs, CO
www.gracepointmatrix.com

For discount copies of this book or bulk ordering,
please contact the publisher at support@GracePointMatrix.com
Printed in the United States of America

TABLE OF CONTENTS

Hi!

I am so excited to welcome you into the Quantum Alignment Family!!

Before you get started exploring the information in this Activation Guide, I wanted to just take a few moments to acknowledge YOU.

If you're like most of my clients, you've spent a lifetime searching for your purpose. You might have a sense of your purpose, or you might be completely unclear about your purpose. However, you know deep in your heart that there is something that you're here to do.

At this point in time, you might even feel some anxiety about your purpose, like it's "pedal to the metal" time as if you're missing the call. You feel compelled to help the world and try to stop some of the suffering—you just don't know you are supposed what to do.

You might also feel like your life isn't a true reflection of your Truth. You might have big broad understandings of concepts (like Universal Love, Abundance, and Consciousness), but still be struggling to make it all work in your life the way you think it "should.". You might be wrestling with your relationships, finding your right work, or even making enough money.

Being human might feel a little challenging some days, even though you know there's more to life than just being a spirit in a body.

We stand on the brink of a powerful time, one heralded by Wise Ones for thousands of years. We are birthing a New World and are in the midst of a huge evolution that is changing the way our intuition works, the way we relate to each other, the way we eat, the way we align ourselves with the Natural World, and more.

Institutions, systems, and businesses that are out of alignment with integrity and the Greater Good are collapsing; we are witnessing the dying gasps of old ideas, pedagogies, and value systems.

It feels disruptive and chaotic. Many of you are super sensitive, feeling this shift deeply in your mind, body, and spirit.

The upheaval we are experiencing is vital. We are making room for a new reality, a new Truth, a world of sustainable resources and peace. YOU play a vital role in creating this New Reality.

You were born at this time for a very special reason, and I am so grateful that you are here, right now, with all of us.

In this Activation Guide, you're going to discover who you are, what you came here to do, how you can stay grounded and present amid upheaval and shift. You're going to learn the mechanics of how your unique energy field operates and your personal strategy for manifesting potential into reality to serve the world in the way your soul longs to do...

This is, obviously, not the only step to changing the world, but it is the first step; it is the step that will align you with new possibilities, quantum creativity, and sustainability.

The world is what it is today because you're in it. It's time you discovered the truth about Who You Truly Are and Why You're Really Here.

From my Heart to Yours,

Karen

GETTING STARTED

1. You'll get the most out of this Activation Guide if you have your Human Design Chart available for reference. To get your chart, go to this link and follow the directions: bit.ly/humandesignchart (We hand calculate our charts to ensure accuracy. It may take up to a day to get your chart to you. Thank you for your patience.)

2. While you're waiting for your chart, you can go ahead and read the Activation Guide. (You're going to remember a lot about what you're here to do right now!)

3. The final section has a series of contemplation/journaling exercises to help you deepen your understanding and activate new meanings in your consciousness. Enjoy!

4. Once you have your chart, please re-read the How to Read Your Chart section of the Activation Guide.

5. Stay tuned. You're going to be getting a series of short video lessons from us to help deepen your understanding of your Life Purpose, the Shift on the planet, and what you can do to optimize your energy to play your part in activating this vital Global Shift.

WHAT'S UP ON THE PLANET RIGHT NOW?

We are standing on the brink of a very important time on this planet. We are on the threshold of heralding the start of a new era, a New Earth. Prophets from many different cultures and times have spoken of this place metaphorically and literally for thousands of years. The details of what is to come have been described with words that are vague, scary, and often ominous. The words of the prophets also offer hope and speak to visions of lasting peace on earth, a time of returning to the garden: Heaven on Earth.

We have a choice to accept a time of suffering and destruction or to take the reins of creation into our hands and become the stewards of a new era for humanity. Either way, we play a powerful role in co-creating with God the world in which we participate. The real question is which destiny will we choose?

We are already running a default program of destruction. We are always creating and (at this point in time) outer appearances would lead us to believe that we may be creating our own destruction. Our conditioning through our human experiences on the planet has created, in most of us, a belief that suffering is a part of being human, that life is hard; we believe we are here to navigate our way through trials and tribulations so that we can redeem our heavenly rewards when we die.

This deep conditioning creates a matrix for fulfillment into form. If we choose to continue to apply these thought forms, then collectively we will most likely create an Earth that is fraught with sparse resources, suffering, and fighting. Read the paper—the evidence is already building.

There are ancient understandings of human power to create a different world that have resurfaced. We are being invited to participate in a new reality that requires us to activate the Divinity in ourselves and to serve as co-creators of a powerful new Earth.

Quantum physics has shown us that Light, which makes us all, travels in pulses and waves. For brief periods of time, two particles of Light can occupy the same space at the same time before diverging onto different paths, creating different realities. These points of contact are Points of Evolution, brief moments when choices and vibrations determine destinies. They are initiated by chaos, periods of reorganization filled with all kinds of experiences from which we may gain clarity.

These seemingly chaotic points of pulsing energy, much like the pulses of a womb contracting to birth new life, are change points that are energized places of choice. Chaos is perceived because, in those moments, there are an infinite number of paths converging simultaneously. For realities to change, meaning to get off one path and onto a different one, there will be the confluence where the two roads meet. We are at such a crucial junction right now. The greater the perceived chaos, the bigger the jump between the two roads and the greater capacity there is for growth.

The true purpose of God and the nature of God is growth. God is always seeking, through us, to expand and grow. Right now, we are being called forth to make a Big Jump, a giant leap in evolution for the world. We all intended to be here on Earth now to be midwives to this process. We are here to grow. This is the most exciting time to be here on this planet. We have been preparing for this time forever!

For us to make the jump in a direction that is joyful and rooted in our consciousness of God, it's going to take a lot of practice and discipline. We are being called upon to release the last threads of belief systems that have kept us separate from our Divinity for lifetimes. These belief systems are so deep and strong that they are rooted into our bodies before we are even born.

The acts of discipline required of us to reprogram our neurobiology have been outlined for us for thousands of centuries. Ancient ones called this discipline Alchemy, though it's not about literally turning lead to gold. This conversion is a metaphor about an intentional participation on a journey to creating Heaven on Earth; it's about taking the dark, unformed blackness of lead and turning it into beautiful, deliberately sculpted pieces of art. You are the artist of your life.

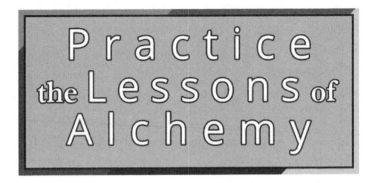

Practice the Lessons of Alchemy

The most powerful teachers in any religion have been Master Alchemists. They have manifested water where there was none, fed multitudes with just a handful of fish as well as a few loaves of bread, and won battles with musical instruments—doing the seemingly impossible with their knowledge and faith. These powerful teachers understood we have contained within us the Divine code for creation.

It is time to listen to our teachers and practice the lessons of Alchemy. We are creating the templates for our future right now. If you are reading this, then your soul is vibrating with an inner longing to make this world a better place. You desire to feel empowered to make a change in your own life and in the lives of others. My intention is to give you some simple insights to help you master the science of Alchemy.

Creation is a logical process. The Universe and God act in an ordered way. Science continues to deepen our understanding of the mechanics of our creative capacities. Our thoughts trigger the manifestation of specific neurotransmitters. These neurotransmitters create an emotional response. Our emotions influence a powerful electromagnetic field in our heart which in turn draws into our lives experiences that match the frequencies of our heart. Once you learn to harness this process consciously, it becomes a predictable formula that you can follow again and again and again.

This is a simple process, but not always easy. The rewards for your determination and perseverance will have a lasting effect on you and leave a legacy for your Earth Brothers and Sisters as well as for our children and their children. We can manifest a delightful New Earth where all souls remember the infinite power of creation that we carry within us.

To stay aligned with your innate creative power, there are 13 Key Disciplines to which you must attend with great consciousness and deliberation. These disciplines take practice, focus, and intention.

You will have days when it feels harder than others. There will be times when you question yourself. This is part of the process; as you go through the lessons, you will learn how to navigate your way through the daily fluctuations of energy.

You are always doing it right. You are always growing and changing. It is truly all good.

13 KEY DISCIPLINES

Release That Which No Longer Serves You

When your hands are full, you can't open them to receive something more unless you let something go. We are conditioned to make do with "less than" and to compromise. Everything you see, hear, smell, touch, and taste in your outer world is simply a metaphorical representation of where you are with your Alchemy and consciousness. Your outer world is always talking to you.

If we consciously settle for "less than," then "less than" will show up everywhere in our lives including our bank accounts, our businesses, and our relationships.

Now is the time to let go of old habits, patterns, thoughts, actions, relationships, jobs, and situations that are no longer in alignment with what you intend to create.

Let Go of Your Past

The past is over. If you allow the stories and excuses from your past to keep you from courageously creating what you want, you are no different than an elephant that is conditioned by the feeling of having a chain around his leg, yet is free to roam.

Do not define yourself by what you have survived. Surviving is less than thriving. Intend to thrive regardless of what has come in your past. Where you put your focus right now is the template for what is to come.

Stay Out of Doubt

Evolution is happening whether we believe it or not. Think about this. What would people have said in the year 1900 about what is taking place on the planet right now? For instance, we are using crystalline and satellite technology to speak to each other all over the world instantly.

While I can sit on the beach in California, my daughter can send me a photo of herself brushing her teeth, and I can reply with a selfie of me feeding seagulls in front of the ocean. I can check emails instantly from a tiny, handheld computer that fits in my pocket.

If everything we see, hear, smell, touch, and taste is simply a metaphorical representation of our alignment with our consciousness, then our technological advances are simply telling us that we are advancing.

Change is happening. More people are waking up and remembering their Divine Magnificence and the power of Alchemy.

You can doubt change and evolution. The truth is that it's going to happen with or without your consciousness. It is Law. We create by thinking and feeling, with a difference between choosing to be a conscious part of the process or choosing to create by default.

Use Fear as Leverage

It's easy to get caught in the sticky web of fear, which can create paralysis and feelings of being "stuck". Physiologically, we see that the experience of fear can shut down thinking and create a survival reaction.

We mistakenly believe that we are experiencing fear in response to change and respond with conditioned paralysis. Most of us are not really experiencing fear. We are instead experiencing resistance. Real fear protects us. Real fear is your intuition telling you not to do something because it might be life-threatening. For example, your fear might tell you to not go into a dark alley at night. This is intuitive and reasonable.

When you are choosing to not make a change because you are afraid, you are not really experiencing fear. You are experiencing resistance or a split in your energy. This kind of "fear" is simply your inner, directional compass letting you know that something in the application of your alchemical process is out of alignment.

If you are feeling resistance it is crucial that you ask yourself these two very important questions:

1. Am I really intending what I truly want or am I intending what I think I should want, what others want me to want, or what I think is possible for me?

2. Do I have beliefs that are keeping me from allowing myself to know that I can have exactly what I intend? (For example, consider if you believe that you must work hard to make money or that for you to get what you want, you might hurt the people you love.)

When you courageously go for what you want with total honesty, complete authenticity, no holds barred no limits... and you believe without a doubt that you can have it, then your resistance magically melts away, and you move forward with enthusiasm and great speed.

Diligently Tend to Your Vibration

At this point in our evolution, the matrix of time is bending and shifting. Speed is increasing. The time between a thought and its manifestation into form is getting shorter and shorter. We cannot afford to be lazy in our intentions and thinking. Yes, our neurobiology and our habits make it easy to fall back on old programming. To make change requires consistent application and discipline.

Your mind is an abundant garden. A garden needs good light, soil, and water to reach its full potential. Tend to the garden of your mind. Give yourself Light and nourishment to help you maximize the potentials of your dreams. Educate yourself. Surround yourself with people who support your creative process. Celebrate your successes. Nurture yourself and allow yourself to receive. Delight in your magnificence. Align yourself with your Divinity.

You are an Unlimited Child of God.

The more you practice, the easier it gets. And the easier it gets, the easier it gets.

Remember Who You Are and Why You Are Here

You are here for a reason. You intended to be here at this time to co-create the future of this world. You are an extremely powerful, unlimited, fully supported Light Being. You have an important role to play in the evolution of this planet. Each and every one of you has a special job here. In this incarnation, you chose a specific energetic blueprint, your Human Design, to help you fulfill your life's mission and purpose.

It is crucial that you understand yourself and who you are so that you can continue to create in alignment with the magnificence of who you intended yourself to be.

Ask for What You Really Want

You WILL get what you ask, but only if it is what you really want. If you are not courageously asking for exactly what you want, your vibration and intentions won't line up behind it, and it won't happen. So many of us right now are walking around frustrated because this "manifesting" thing doesn't seem to be working. If what you are intending isn't really what you are wanting—if your seeming desire is a compromise, an obligation, or even if it isn't big enough—you will struggle to get enough energy rolling to create the momentum for creation.

Part of the experience here on the planet right now is not so much about creating the things we desire as much as it is about creating a vibration of joy and delight as well as gaining the experience of mastering the power of Alchemy. We must master Alchemy, as we will be called on to co-create on a global level to change the collective matrix. If we are to collectively choose a destiny for this planet, we must be experienced, conscious creators.

Pray for Your Evolution Every Day

This shift on the planet requires discipline. We cannot afford to spend energy focusing on the things, which we do not like about our world, as we know it, or we will create that which we are seeking to eliminate from our experience.

To stay aligned on the cutting-edge of consciousness, it is crucial that you set a daily intention to vibrate in alignment with the high vibrations of joy, delight, and love. When you pray, see yourself manifesting the exact experiences and support you need to help you clarify your intentions and maintain your vibrational alignment with that which you desire.

Practice, Practice, Practice

There is no moment in your day or night that is not a spiritual moment. All moments, intentions and actions are spiritual. You are an infinite Light Being experiencing a human perception as a small component of the total aspect of who you really are. It takes practice to live the human life and blend it with the larger aspect of your Divinity.

We are so used to living in a way that is unconscious and haphazard. To implement deliberate, intention-based living takes practice. Alchemy is a new skill, and you will have to practice repeatedly, which is not any different than being a musician. We are all born with the potential to be musicians just like we are all born with the potential to be powerful alchemists. It takes time and practice to make a good musician, just as it takes time and practice to make a good alchemist.

Create Community

While making changes in your vibration and mindset ultimately is a personal journey that you must take alone, your outer reality can profoundly influence your inner reality, too. Frequencies modulate. The more you attract and align with others of similar intent and vibration, the faster you will all progress.

Now is a time of deep community. We will be called upon to unite in consciousness to shift our collective beliefs and the collective projection of the planetary matrix. We are not here on this journey to be alone. We are here to create a new world together. We must align ourselves energetically to project vibration of the matrix of Heaven here on Earth.

Now is the time to practice co-creating unified goals and intentions together. When we come together in groups of two or more with the intention to create a deliberate experience we amplify our energies and our opportunities for growth.

Be Honest and Authentic

As a creator, you cannot create from a dishonest intention. Your underlying belief and motive for your dishonesty will somehow manifest, usually as chaos. It is Law. You are either going to get caught in your dishonesty because you are afraid of being caught and you focus on it, or you will get caught because your underlying desire is to be authentic.

If your actions and words are not authentic, and if you are not fully intending what you are saying, there will be no manifestation. Your ultimate responsibility is to live true to yourself and your desires, with the understanding that when you live true to yourself, you live in alignment with God and your motivations will be to harm no others.

You cannot be responsible for other people's reactions to your truth. You cannot deny who you are or your purpose because of your fear that you may hurt others. You will ultimately hurt them more with your dishonesty. You cannot control the feelings or reactions of others, although you can control your experience with others

You are perfectly created to assume a role in the evolution of the planet. When you step away from the authentic calling of your soul, you walk away from your potential points of contact that will allow you to create destinies with integrity. Honestly, sometimes when we are not acting authentically, we miss opportunities to evolve and keep others from growing as well. We are not here to be heroes or martyrs, nor are we here to suffer.

Let Go of the Ropes

For lifetimes we have been conditioned to be prepared, just in case. In the evolving times to come, the cataclysmic nature of potential events may be so unexpected that there will be no preparing. This is why mastering Alchemy is so vital because when you master Alchemy, you can always use intention and your vibrational alignment to know how to navigate through unpredictable situations.

Alchemy prepares the way for constant and everyday miracles. When you understand the Laws and the physics of the Universe, you know that you can never fall or fail; you are always fully supported, and the full blueprint for creation is within you.

Faith and trust are like muscles. They need to be strengthened with exercise and practice. Practice Alchemy until you are a master. Let go and trust that when you are in alignment with your Life Purpose and your Divine Blueprint, you will be fully supported.

Be Deliberate and Remember Choice

There is not a single moment when you do not have control over your experience even though you may not be able to change actual events. There are some events that have been scripted into your journey since before you got here. You do have control over how you will experience all circumstances.

If you choose to focus on what you do like and what is good about a situation (as difficult as it may be), you will ultimately have a deeply different experience than if you are resisting and pushing against situations. When the heat is high, and your experience seems too challenging and difficult, stop, and redirect your focus on what you want to be experiencing, what you desire to feel in the situation. Hold your attention and emotions in that place to the best of your ability.

It may seem counterintuitive at this point, but I restate *that on which you focus grows*. If you want to change your experience, you must change your focus. Look at the good in your situation and keep your focus on your desired outcome.

It's up to you.

Excerpted from Inside the Body of God, 13 Strategies for Thriving in the New World by Karen Curry Parker

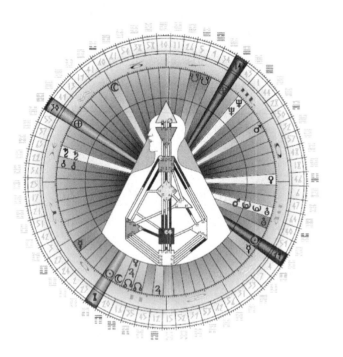

QUANTUM CREATIVITY

It can feel despairing, overwhelming, and power-less to read the news and to feel like you aren't able to DO anything to change or help what's happening on the planet. You may feel like donating money or supplies isn't enough. Your heart is hurting for the world every time you read the news.

I want to share something with you that I hope will inspire you to feel more aligned and empowered in the face of the turbulent energies we're experiencing on the planet. You have the power to add to the creation of sustainability and peace in the world; you play a vital role in healing the planet.

We are facing some powerful challenges on this planet, and the intense weather has opened our eyes to the immediacy of what's potentially facing us if we don't engineer some innovative solutions. Besides the basic things like shelter, water, food, and access to healthcare (which, of course, are VITAL for people), the world needs two very important things that you can give it:

- **Creativity.**
- **Sustainability.**

I want to break these two things down for you and explain them in greater depth because I believe that what I am sharing with you is the most important thing for you to understand right now. When you understand this powerful information, you will be able to be who you came here to be so that you can do what you came here to do.

Creativity is a word that terrifies many of us. We associate "creativity" with artistic ability or expressive capacities. Some of you may even have memories of feeling like you weren't "good at art" or other such nonsense. However, those connotations aren't quite accurate. Creativity is the ability to find solutions.

When you pack your kids lunch, you are being creative. When you get a stain out of your shirt, you are being creative. When you find a new way to get to work that avoids traffic, you are being creative. When you find new ways to communicate with your loved ones that are more respectful and honoring, you are being creative. When you discover ways to empower yourself and grow in your self-esteem, you are being creative. You get the point.

You are creating every second of your existence.

You ARE creative.

Situational Creativity vs. Fundamental Creativity

There are two kinds of creativity: situational creativity and fundamental creativity.

Situational Creativity is:

- In the moment.
- Reactive.
- Determined by your conditioning (your beliefs, your experiences, your epigenetic lineage, your Human Design, etc.).
- Offers short-term solutions.
- Finite - comes from the conditioned mind.
- The result of "thinking" and "reasoning" (The Mind).
- "Reasonable."

Situational creativity is limited to what we think is probable and possible. It's also based on what we believe is true and rooted in our past experiences. It does not allow us to be open to new solutions and innovations because it's very limited and reactive.

21

Let's look at an example of situational creativity. Let's say that you have a consistent struggle with money in your life. Maybe you have a pattern where every time you make extra money, something happens to wipe out any extra money you may have made. (Maybe your car broke down, or you got an unexpected tax bill, something like that.)

That repeated pattern conditions you to expect that any time you have extra money, is that something bad will happen to cause you to lose your extra money. In response to this conditioning, you create a situationally creative response - you immediately spend the extra money so that you don't "lose" it again. You don't save your extra money or invest in building a financial foundation. You also lose your trust in abundance and financial prosperity.

When faced with the seemingly overwhelming challenges on the planet right now, it's easy for us to fall into situationally creative responses. We have been told by the media, in movies, and even by scientists that we are doomed. Just one example is that climate change will decimate the planet and many people will starve and struggle.

Our media and even the entertainment industry salivate over stories of destruction and movies about post-apocalyptic worlds. We are conditioned to think that our situation is "impossible" and that there is nothing we can do about it. We react with fear, despair, and even fail to act because we think it won't help anyway.

Let me just remind you that there was once a time when people thought it was "impossible" to go to the moon or prevent diseases like polio. The creative solutions to polio or to getting to the moon didn't happen until people began to believe it was possible. The very first and MOST important thing that we can do right now from the comfort of our homes is to begin to shift our beliefs about what we think is possible. (And then, of course, take inspired action!)

The second kind of creativity called **Fundamental Creativity**. There are several attributes to this different kind of creativity because it:

- Transcends conditioning.
- Usually arrives in the form of an epiphany ("Ah-ha!").
- Comes from the Quantum Field and is unlimited by our finite minds.
- Is imaginative and possibility oriented.
- Aligns with Cosmic Order (in other words it's aligned with LOVE).
- Is "un-reasonable."

Fundamental Creativity has given us things like electricity, the capacity to go to the moon, combustion engines, and more!

We are designed to tap into evolutionary fundamental creativity. It's our nature and part of our hard-wiring. But our training in life has taught us to experience creativity only

23

within the limits of what we think is possible and that, if we want to create something new, we must "figure it out."

Think about this for a minute. How many times have you struggled and wrestled with a problem and then suddenly had an epiphany in the shower after weeks of worry, stress, and twisting your brain? Shower epiphanies are experiences of Fundamental Creativity.

If we're going to solve the challenges of the world, we have to do two things. We must shift what we believe is possible and we have to deepen our capacity to become more fundamentally creative.

To become more fundamentally creative and to be ready to receive the creative "sparks" that will give us the solutions to creating a sustainable and peaceful world, we have to:

1. De-Condition ourselves. (We must release pain, trauma, and change our epigenetic programming that keeps us from believing in seemingly impossible solutions.)

2. Know who we are. (Self-knowledge and self-awareness is the best defense against getting caught up in the Group Mindset of lack, despair, and the idea of "impossible.")

Our brains give us our best ideas when:

1. A lot of dopamine is released in our system. Triggers like exercising, listening to music, and,

yes, taking a warm shower contribute to increased dopamine flow.

2. We are relaxed. When we have a relaxed state of mind, we're more likely to turn attention inwards, able to make insightful connections. We've seen before how being drunk and sleepy are great for creativity.

3. We are distracted. Distraction gives our brains a break so our subconscious can work on a problem more creatively. (This is similar to John Cleese's advice to let your ideas bake.)

A dopamine high, relaxed state, and distracted mind: No wonder great ideas happen in the shower.

In other words, taking care of yourself, staying connected to beauty, well-being, truth, love, and other archetypes that are more aligned with creativity as well as managing stress will support you in finding solutions to change the world.

You have within you the capacity to generate an innumerable number of possible solutions to help the world and to face the challenges in your own life. But you can't access these solutions if you're reacting from a conditioned place, if you're freaked out, worried, or feeling despair.

Your creative response to life increases when you are living a life that is aligned with your authentic self and when you are taking care of yourself. It's from that place that you are able to serve the world better.

ARE YOU SUSTAINABLE?

In the last section, I posed the questions:
"What can we do in the face of tragedy and extreme circumstances? How can we help the world?"

I wrote about how the world needs to major things right now:

1. **Quantum Creativity.**
2. **Sustainability.**

In this section, I want to share with you how to become "sustainable" and why it's so vital for YOU and for the world right now. And we must start this conversation with the definition of sustainability. Sustainability is the ability to endure and thrive no matter what is happening around you. It's also the ability to have access to all the resources you need to sustain yourself and your loved ones.

The world is facing a crisis of sustainability right now. Or, at least we think it is.

Scientists are telling us that with global warming, we are losing the ability to grow crops and to feed the world at its current population level. There are people currently on the planet who are experiencing the reality of this in their daily lives due to extreme weather events on the planet.

We are told that to become sustainable and to try to stave off some of the effects of global warming as well as environmental destruction that we need to go "green." We are told that we need to enact drastic measures to align our choices with what the planet and her inhabitants can endure.

Let's have an honest conversation about this for a moment.

How many of you are following through on a "green" lifestyle?

Have you given up your car, bike everywhere, converted your home to solar, only eat organic fruits and veggies, eat vegan, only buy items in bulk, and use only cloth grocery bags?

Do you only have what you need in your life and nothing more?

Do you compost everything, have your own garden, and only buy used items?

Most of us are only doing a couple of these things. It's kind of like taking your vitamins or working out, right? You know you should do it, but you don't always do it the way you think you should in your mind.

Here's the next set of uncomfortable questions. Ready?

How many of you give whatever extra you have to others?

How many of you give away more than you can afford to and end up martyring yourself for the sake of others?

How many of you fail to set good boundaries and honor your own personal value?

And…

How many of you create sustainability in your relationships with other people on the planet?

Do you sometimes judge others?

Do you feel the internal push to "get your fair share"?

Do you feel the need to be "right"?

How much do you overcompensate and justify doing things you know you "shouldn't" because you're exhausted, burned out, frustrated, angry, disappointed, or bitter about your life on some level? How much have you compromised in your life?

I know that sometimes these questions can be difficult or even trigger a defense reaction. That's not my intention, but I invite you to really feel your answers to these questions. Your answers will help you understand just how sustainable you are being in the world.

I would very gently and lovingly suggest that very few of us are actually being sustainable in the world. I'm not saying this to make you feel guilty. If you're reading this, odds are you are way more sustainable than the average person on the planet. We need to do better.

The number one source of pain (and lack of sustainability) that I've seen in my clients over the past 28 years is lack of alignment with the Authentic Self.

When you are compromising what you really want in your life, when you say "no" to things to which you want to say "yes" (and vice versa), when you believe that it's impossible to do/be/have what you want in your life, when you forget who you are and why you are here, it creates a whole set of painful consequences.

If you've never learned to be Who You Truly Are or it was unsafe or not allowed for you to express your Authentic Self, you will most likely: exhibit several signs:

Signs of Compromise

- Question your lovability
- Feel powerless
- Question your value
- Burn out
- Lose connection with your Quantum Creativity and your Inner Wisdom
- Make emotional decisions that you regret
- Suppress what you want and need
- Let fear rule your life
- Struggle to make good decisions for yourself

If you are experiencing any of these, it will be hard for you to make sustainable choices. For example, let's say you question your value and you experience low self-esteem. When you have low self-esteem, you might not do the things you need to do to take care of yourself. You may justify doing things that aren't good for you because unconsciously you feel like you "don't matter anyway."

Or, let's say you are burned out. You're most likely not going to go to the gym, take the extra steps to make a compost pile in your backyard, or streamline your life to make it more effective and efficient. You simply don't have the energy. You may even feel like you should fight for resources in your life because you are afraid that you might not have the energy to do what you need to do when the time is right. Maybe you hoard or hold back because you're afraid you'll only deepen your experience of burnout. If you are experiencing any of these symptoms above, you will not be living sustainably, and you won't have the energy to create sustainably on the planet.

Not only that but if you are not living true to yourself, you probably have carefully crafted an identity that is "more acceptable" and "fits in" better with what you think the world will allow for you. You may be denying what is Truth for you because you think it's safe or maybe the only way to experience success in life. Anytime we craft an identity that is not true to Who We Really Are, we are burning excess energy. It takes a lot of energy to be someone or something you're not. Eventually, you will burn out simply because you can't maintain the lie anymore.

However, we do have hope. The energy for sustainable resources in Human Design is contained in the following flow of energies. When you are aligned with Who You Truly Are, you save yourself a tremendous amount of energy and this alignment makes you more available to all the good, joyful, and juicy things in life. It also gives you more energy to be sustainable in the world. The world needs more of that right now.

The world also needs you to be more of YOU right now.

WHAT (YOU) AND THE WORLD NEED NOW

In my previous two sections, you learned about the importance of activating your Quantum Creativity and why being aligned with your Authentic Self is vital, not only for your health, abundance, spiritual connection, Life Purpose, and your relationships but also for the world. You also learned that Sustainability is crucial to helping the world thrive during this time of massive upheaval. When you are living from a place that is not aligned with your Authentic Self, you waste energy trying to hold on to an identity that isn't true to Who You Really Are. When you waste your energy that way, it makes it hard for you to act in sustainable ways and make sustainable choices.

Not only is living from your Authentic Self vital to maintaining sustainable energy and fundamental creativity for YOU and the planet but living from your Authentic Self is crucial to activating abundance and prosperity in every area of your life. (...So, you can have more...and you can give more...) In addition to being creative and sustainable, the world desperately needs us to be fully activating our abundance.

Let's look at the Human Design chart to define the word "abundance." Human Design (a synthesis of Eastern and Western Astrology, the Chinese I' Ching, the Hindu Chakra System, Judaic Kabbalah, and Quantum Physics) is a synthesis of many different cultural archetypes. It's a modern way to look at the different components of the human potential. The energy for "abundance" is rooted in the Gate 55, which is called the Gate of Abundance in Human Design. In the Human Design chart, abundance is defined as the emotional frequency of energy that supports your awareness of Spirit as the Source of all there is. (Don't worry if your chart doesn't look the one below. Everyone's chart is unique, and we will be diving into areas of your personal chart later. I am talking about the chart in general and merely showing you that the blueprint for being human includes a natural hardwiring for abundance)

In other words, to become "abundant," you must have faith that you will be provided for and that FAITH is what aligns you with the energy of Abundance. Abundance is an emotional energy that is connected ultimately to the Heart. The Gate of Abundance energetically synchronizes with the magnetic resonance field of your Heart to influence what you attract into your life. The more you carry an abundant vibration, the more your Heart attracts abundance into your life.

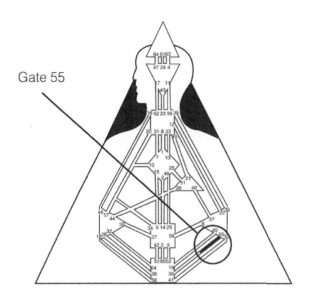

Gate 55

We create with the energy of the Gate 55 when we feel "good" and when we Trust in Abundance. The Gate 55 is physiologically associated with digestion and assimilation, the pancreas and emotional eating. We are designed to have and consume/eat "enough." If we eat too much or we don't have enough food, it's unhealthy. We are hard-wired to need just enough to stay satiated. (If you are not aligned with your abundance, or you struggle with faith, it's also natural to reach for food - especially sugar- to try to fill the emotional void you experience when you feel disconnected from Source.)

To me, the energy of the Gate 55 begs a new definition for what it means to be abundant. I believe that sometimes in the Western World, we define abundance in an extreme and lavish way. The overabundance of energy that it takes to maintain and sustain more than enough material goods is another way that we deplete ourselves and create internal anxiety. (Think about how energizing it feels to clear your clutter and to get rid of things you don't need.)

As we dive deeper into the Human Design chart, you will see that not only are we designed to be abundant, but that abundance in the chart is not associated with work. We are abundant because we exist. It's our natural state when we are living True to Who We Are.

Abundance is sufficiency - having enough - not less than and not more. To create an abundant world, we have to make peace with the idea of sufficiency. Somehow in our experience of abundance, we feel deprived if we don't have more than enough. Sufficiency has somehow gotten a bad rap like it's bad to have "only" enough.

Many ancient texts teach us about faith and sufficiency. In the Old Testament, the People of Israel escape from slavery in Egypt and are sent to wander in the desert looking for a new place to settle. They are frightened, have no food or water and don't know what to do. In response to their worry, God lays out a powerful plan to teach them to trust in sufficiency. God tells them not to be afraid, that each day they will be given enough food in the form of a special substance called Manna.

God explains to them that they can gather just what they need every day. If they gather more than what they need, the extra will rot. If their neighbor can't gather their share for some reason, they may gather extra for their neighbor and give it to them. God also tells them that on the sixth day they will be given a double portion so that they can rest.

This story is a powerful metaphor for the Gate 55. If we can live in the vibration of abundance that is described in the story of Manna, then it is easy and natural for us to take what we need and share the rest. We must learn to be gracious and grateful for the sufficiency that we have and to not overcompensate from a place of imaginary lack when we use and share our resources.

Buckminster Fuller, a philanthropist and cultural visionary, once said that there are enough resources on the planet for five billion people to become millionaires. I believe that this is still true - even though there are now more people on the planet. We all have the potential to become millionaires and live abundant and thriving lives. Our problem isn't that we don't have enough to go around. Our challenge is learning how to allocate and share what we have in a way that honors the value of each one of us.

We can't do that unless we believe that we ourselves are worthy of "enough;" we can't do that if our own personal energy is depleted and if we are disconnected from our own awareness and worthiness of being in our natural flow of sufficiency, support, and abundance.

It's part of our hard-wiring and our natural state to have enough for ourselves and to share. We need to remember that part of our True Identity.

THE ENERGY FLOW FOR
SUSTAINABLE RESOURCES

We are hard-wired and designed to be sustainable. You can find the requirements and the energy for sustainable resources in the Human Design chart. (By the way, we ALL have ALL of the energies in the chart. It doesn't matter if you have it "open" or "defined." The stuff that's colored or white in in the chart only tells you whether you experience that particular energy consistently or in a variety of ways. The information I am sharing is about the blueprint of the human potential and applies to all of us.)

The energy for sustainable resources is contained in the following flow of energy in the chart. These energies are strictly about material resources. (ALL humans are more energetically sustainable when they are living a life that is the full expression of their Authentic Self.)

The major nexus in the chart for sustainable resources is the Will Center. This is the energy Center that is responsible for manifesting on the material plane. The Will Center contains the energy for money, material goods, and the will to allocate as well as manage resources so that they will endure and be sustainable.

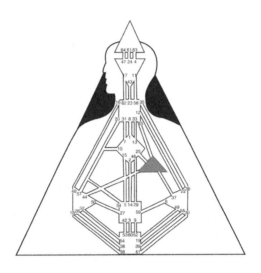

It is the home of "Will power"—we can push and force with our will to create. The interesting thing about Will energy is that most of us don't have consistent access to Will power. In addition, and probably ironically, the most powerful way to tap into "will" is to surrender. It's in the Will Center that we learn to surrender the "ego" to your Higher Self and serve something greater than our individual selves. It's also where we have to let go of our personal will and allow (surrender) to the flow of abundance, to trust that it will appear in sufficient ways, and to master the will to wait for right timing and alignment.

The right timing and alignment of the Will not only happens when we surrender and let go; it only happens when we are well rested. The Will Center "knows" when you don't have the energy to do what you need to do to create something, so your creative process tends to "stall out," sometimes leaving you feeling betrayed by God or deeply frustrated and exhausted. It is that state of exhaustion and burnout that often forces us to surrender so that the right thing can unfold in our lives. Sometimes, we must defeat our own will to allow the flow of abundance to finally reach us.

We are hardwired for action AND rest. In fact, scientists have shown that the nature of not only humans but also of the Universe is to expand (push) and then contract (rest). Movement and repose are how abundance flows. It's not a faucet that is constantly running, requiring us to tend to it with power and energy. It's a cyclical energy that has built into it cycles of rest and restoration so that we can take care of ourselves without being depleted and exhausted. To be fully abundant, you must take consistent cycles of deep rest and stay energized by letting go.

Secondly, the Will Center is the seat of self-worth in the chart. Most of us have to learn the true value of who we are individually. We cannot allow "enough" for ourselves when we do not think we are worthy of "enough." If you don't value yourself, you will push away resources that are intended for you to sustain yourself...so that you can, in turn, sustain others.

Unhealthy Will energy often manifests in two destructive ways: martyrdom or hoarding. When we don't believe in our own value, we give everything away in an attempt to prove our worth. This endless giving leaves us depleted and without our own resources, eventually taking us out of the True flow of abundance. We can also do the opposite and hoard resources because we're afraid we're not worthy of receiving more and we shut down the flow of abundance not only to ourselves but to others. Obviously, both strategies aren't sustainable. Of course, it's also hard to believe in "enough" when you question whether you are "enough."

The third thing that the Will Center tells us about sustainability is that we cannot be sustainable when we act alone. We are designed to be part of community; we need community to support and sustain us. It also means that to be sustainable we must rely on others, ask for help, and be available for others in the same way. This is a fierce and vital connection that we share. We cannot be abundant if we are not ALL abundant.

The Will Center also shows us that sustainability comes from integrity, not only moralistic integrity but "structural" integrity. If we are to endure the challenges, the ebbs, and flows of life, we must be in alignment with our authentic self and do the Right Thing. Lack of integrity might result in short-term gain, but in the end, it is not sustainable. Not only that, under the current celestial influences, lack of moralistic integrity is causing old systems that deal with managing and allocating resources to disintegrate, making room for something better.

Last, but not least, the Will Center shows us that we are designed to "manage" the material plain and material goods. It's not enough to visualize an Abundant New World. Of course, imagining is a vital first step, but we have to do the work of the world. In the third dimension, we get things done by action. We must hand out water and food, provide shelter, protect the innocent, create schools, and allocate the resources we have so that we all can have what we need to survive and thrive.

INTRODUCTION TO YOUR QUANTUM BLUEPRINT: YOUR HUMAN DESIGN

The moment of your conception marked an important, once-in-a-lifetime event. At that moment the Universe joined your soul with a powerful story, the story of your life. The story of You is so unique that it has never been on the planet before and it will never be on the planet again.

Over the course of your life, you may have forgotten your story. You may have been told that you "should" be a certain way, act a certain way and that there are key formulas that you have to follow to be successful or healthy. If you're like most people, you may have struggled to make the rules you were given fit or work for you. You may have followed the rules very well and still not gotten the results for which you were hoping. Your journey may have left you feeling depleted and not good enough. You may have lost touch with the powerful story of Who You Truly and felt that there is something wrong with you.

There is nothing wrong with you! You just forgot Who You Truly Are!

It makes sense that if you are a once-in-a-lifetime event in this Universe that there are no "formulas" for health and vitality, abundance, right relationship, right work, or success in life other than the ones that work for you. There is no one-size-fits-all approach to creating success. In fact, even the definition of success is unique to each one of us.

The greatest source of pain in life is the disconnect from our authentic self - the real story of Who You Truly Are. When we try to squeeze the powerful essence of who we are behind masks or into small definitions of who we should be, it unleashes a subtle restlessness inside of us. This subtle restlessness creates stress and unhappiness, an inner awareness that you're not living your life purpose or being true to yourself and a sense that there's more to the story.

Human Design is a powerful tool to help you remember your story. Based on a synthesis of Eastern and Western Astrology, the Chinese I 'Ching, the Hindu Chakra System, Kabbalah, and Quantum Physics, this powerful system shows you your strengths, your purpose, your gifts and gives you a map to help you realign your life with the true story of Who You Truly Are.

This Introduction is designed to jog your memory, to push against that inner restlessness that you may feel and to help you answer the most important question in the world: Who are you?

May the words in this begin the start of your journey back to remembering Who You Truly Are.

The next section of this Activation Guide is broken into two parts:

1. **An Introduction to the Parts of the Chart** is a short technical definition of what you see in your Human Design chart. The intention for this section is to simply help you navigate your way through all the data and images listed on your chart.

2. **Putting it All Together and Keeping It Simple** is a short summary of the important parts of the chart and what you need to focus on to get the most out of your introduction to your Human Design Chart.

AN INTRODUCTION TO THE PARTS OF THE CHART

Your Human Design Chart is made of two distinctly different aspects: your Soul Purpose and your Life Purpose. The purpose of life is growth and expansion. Our souls manifest on Earth to experience whatever they need to experience to add the growth of the Universe.

Your Life Purpose is the story of the who you are in this incarnation. This story is encoded in your energy blueprint as well as in your genetic and epigenetic lineage. At the moment of your birth, you Soul Purpose integrated with your Life Purpose to create the once-in-a-lifetime event that is YOU!

Over our lives, we often experience struggle between elements of our Soul Purpose and our Life Purpose. These inner struggles are often "pre-scripted" into the story of your life. Many people find that when they really understand their Human Design, they gain a deeper understanding of their own inner struggles. This awareness helps you gain new levels of self-mastery so that you can fulfill your potential in a richer, more meaningful way.

Understanding the Chart

The Human Design chart, called the Body Graph, is a visual representation of the sum of human possibilities and energies. The entire archetype of humanity is contained within the structural framework of the chart. All the possibilities for the expression of being human appear here. The Body Graph shows us the different ways we love, hate, lead, follow, learn, know, grow and so much more!

Not only that, the chart shows your best strategy for making money, having great relationships, being healthy and staying creatively fulfilled. Your unique chart helps you understand how you work and how to best make your life work for you.

One the next page is a sample chart. Your chart will look different based on the tool used to generate the chart and your unique expression represented in the chart.

Each individual chart (calculated using your birth date, time, and place) is a "map" of how you process energy. The chart reveals your strengths, your potential weaknesses, your gifts as well as your talents. Most importantly, the chart tells the story of who you are, why you are here, and how you can live a life that is true to who you really are.

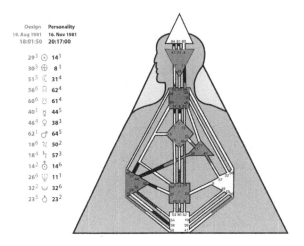

Design | Personality
19. Aug 1981 | 16. Nov 1981
18:01:50 | 20:17:00

29³	☉	14¹
30³	⊕	8¹
51⁵	☾	31⁴
56⁶	☊	62⁴
60⁶	☋	61⁴
40¹	☿	44⁵
46⁴	♀	38³
62¹	♂	64⁵
18⁶	♃	50²
18⁴	♄	57³
14²	♅	14⁶
26⁶	♆	11¹
32²	☉	32⁶
23⁵	♇	23²

Overview

Type: Generator

    Conditioning Theme: Frustration

    Strategy: Wait to Respond

Profile: 1/3, Investigating Martyr

    14-8 / 29-30: The right angle cross of Contagion(4)

    Right angle - Personal Destiny

Definition: Triple Split Definition

Inner Authority: Sacral Expressed Generated

The story of each chart is based on the synthesis of everything in the chart. Each one is different and unique. It's in the sum total of all the parts of the chart that your personal energy "map" is revealed.

Human Design is rich and complex; it involves a lot of data. The system is a synthesis of Eastern and Western Astrology, the Chinese I 'Ching, the Kabbalah, the Hindu Chakra System and quantum physics.

If you look at the chart closely, you might find visual evidence of some of the "parts" of Human Design. For example, if you turn the chart upside down, it looks very similar to the Tree of Life from the Judaic Kabbalah.

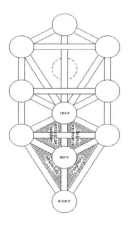

Or you may notice that there are 64 numbers that appear on the Body Chart. These numbers, called Gates, correlate to the 64 Hexagrams from the Chinese I 'Ching.

And, there are nine geometric shapes ("Centers") that appear on different parts of the body, similar to the seven energy centers of the Hindu Chakra system.

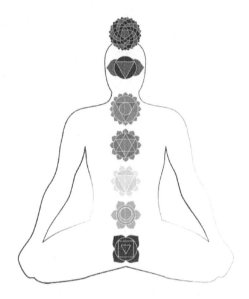

Even though you can see pieces of these ancient wisdom teachings in the chart, Human Design, in and of itself, is something new and unique. It's a brand-new tool to help people in a brand-new way.

Pulling all the information together in synthesis is key to understanding Human Design as well as each individual chart. At its root, Human Design is a tool that teaches us about the power and possibility of evolution in mankind. There are learnings on a personal, relationship and collective level. The real beauty of Human Design is truly in the unification of all its unique esoteric components.

The actual chart is also a synthesis of several parts that play together to give an overview of each individual. To "see" the big picture of a chart and to make learning about Human Design easier, we must start first with taking the chart apart, piece by piece. Let's break down the parts of the chart into their individual components so you can begin to understand how the different pieces fit together.

Some of the individual pieces of the chart have energies that are similar but are actually different on a subtle level. Please understand as you learn about each part that we are (to a certain degree) taking pieces of the chart out of context. Each piece is important, but the full expression of each part will depend on what else is in your unique chart.

The Nine Energy Centers

The first thing you will notice when you look at your chart is that there are nine geometric shapes. These shapes are called the nine Centers. Each Center carries and manages a certain frequency of energy and relates to specific themes in our lives.

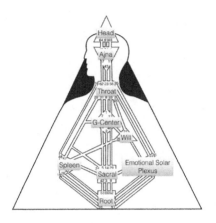

As you can see from the image, the Centers are: Head, Ajna, Throat, G-Center (Identity/Self) Will, Spleen, Sacral, Emotional Solar Plexus, Sacral, and Root. If a Center is colored, then it is called Defined. A Defined Center has a consistent way of operating and is part of who you are. This is the energy that you radiate out into the world. It operates the same way energetically and thematically.

If a Center is white, then it is called Undefined or "open". Open Centers are where we take in energy and information from the world around us. Not only do we absorb energies in our open Centers, we also amplify them. In our open Centers, we experience other people's energies. It is in these open Centers that we have the potential for great wisdom, but also the potential for pain and confusion.

Your defined Centers represent aspects of your personality that are consistent and true about you all the time. It can be raining, Mercury can be in retrograde, Mars can disappear out of the solar system, but your definition always stays the same.

Undefined areas represent aspects of your personality that are inconsistent. Where you are undefined is where you take energy and information from other people. Not only do you absorb it, you amplify it.

For example, if you have an undefined emotional solar plexus (the triangle on the lower right-hand side of the body graph), you absorb other people's emotions, and you feel them stronger than the person actually generating the feelings. Emotionally undefined individuals are empathic. With awareness, this empathy can be a great source of wisdom. Any center where you are undefined is potentially a great source of wisdom.

To illustrate my point, let me give you an example. I have an undefined emotional solar plexus. I hate going to movies because I bawl my eyes out every time. When I watched the movie, "Spirit, Stallion of the Cimarron" (an animated movie about a horse), I cried so hard during the whole movie that my nine-year-old daughter got up and moved to another seat because she was so embarrassed by my behavior. Honestly, it wasn't THAT sad a movie. What I now understand is that my open emotional system was taking in all the emotional energy in the theater and amplifying it. I was crying the tears for the people in the whole theater.

While not helpful at a movie, it is critical in my life. In my coaching practice, this aspect of being emotionally undefined is a great asset for me. When I am assessing my client's emotional status, I KNOW what they are feeling because I am feeling it, too!

In another example, when I worked as a nurse, this was very exhausting for me because I didn't understand my Human Design. I burned out very quickly because the emotional intensity was overwhelming and I would soak it up like a sponge. Now I use my emotional solar plexus as a screen, allowing all of that emotional information to pass through me. I don't hold on to it (meaning claiming it as my own), and I don't burn out.

Children who are emotionally undefined sometimes get labeled as being "dramatic". What they are doing is taking in all the emotional energy from the people around them and acting it out. I often see emotionally undefined children labeled as "disturbed" when they are, in fact, acting out the emotional health of their family or even emotional drama in their parent's marriage.

The beauty in the defined and undefined Centers and lies in the fact that individually we are all simply puzzle pieces -- parts of a greater whole. We all become completely defined when we are all together. We each bring pieces that energetically unify us all and offer us the opportunity to express all the human experience.

You sense this when you go to a restaurant or a coffee shop. The designs of the customers and the staff blend together to make a collective aura.

Your definition comes from the position of the Gates and the planets at the moment of your birth. Wherever you have open energy in your chart, you take it in from the collective aura of the others in the coffee shop. Your energy and your definition (colored in parts of your chart) interact with other people's energy and definition. You are imprinted with other people's energies wherever you have openness in your chart. We can look at how the Body Chart and Centers integrate with your Conscious and Unconscious Birthday in the next section.

The Numbers and Planets
on the Chart

On the left-hand side of the chart or flanking either side of the body graph (depending on which software you used to receive your free Human Design chart), you will see a series of red and black numbers along with planetary symbols.

You might also see that there are two birthdates located on your chart. The birth date in black is your actual birthday, called your Conscious Birthday in Human Design. (On some charts, the birthday may be in European format, i.e., day/month/year.) The red birthday is called your Unconscious Birthday.

Two Birthdates

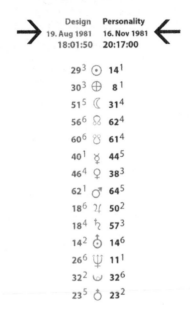

Design	Personality
19. Aug 1981	16. Nov 1981
18:01:50	20:17:00

29^3	☉	14^1
30^3	⊕	8^1
51^5	☾	31^4
56^6	♌	62^4
60^6	☊	61^4
40^1	☿	44^5
46^4	♀	38^3
62^1	♂	64^5
18^6	♃	50^2
18^4	♄	57^3
14^2	♅	14^6
26^6	♆	11^1
32^2	♇	32^6
23^5	☋	23^2

The numbers in **BLACK** are calculated on your actual birthday. This is called your Conscious Design. Your Conscious Design contains the information that tells you about your Soul Purpose. The elements on the chart that are black are aspects of your personality of which you are consciously aware and, to a certain degree, over which you have some control.

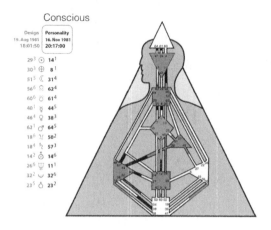

The Unconscious Birthday (the one in **RED**) is calculated approximately 88 astrological degrees from the moment of your birth (roughly three months prior to your birth). The Red parts of the chart contain the information about your Life Purpose and what you're here to learn. This is the design of your Unconscious Personality.

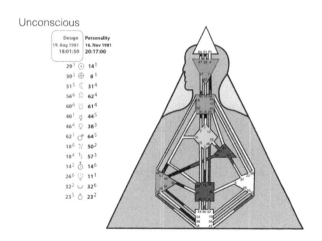

Your Unconscious Design Personality is defined by the red elements on the chart and represents aspects of your personality that are consistently part of who you are but are unconscious. This means you don't really have much control over these parts of your personality. Usually, with age, we become more aware of our Unconscious Personality, and we learn to fulfill our Life Purpose in a more mature way. Your family and loved ones also usually know the Unconscious elements of who you are much sooner than you do yourself.

The planetary symbols indicate the astrological position of the energies in your chart at the moment of your birth. Your birth chart - the numbers alongside your Body Graph - is fixed and does not change during your whole life.

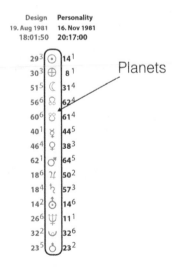

Design   **Personality**
19. Aug 1981   16. Nov 1981
18:01:50   20:17:00

Planets

The Channels

The next thing that you may notice on your chart is that it is covered with lines, some of them colored red, some black, some checkered black/red, and some white.

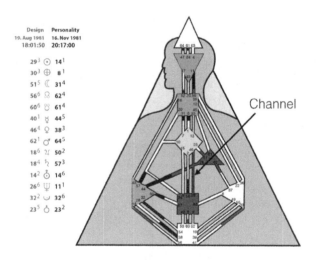

Lines that span all the way between two Centers and are a combination of white, red, black, or checkered, are called Channels. If you have a line that is colored to both ends (either solid or checkered), then the Centers on either end of the Channel will be defined (colored). An open (white) center has no fully colored channels attached to it.

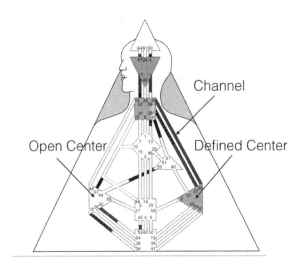

When only one Gate in a Channel is defined, it is called a Hanging Gate:

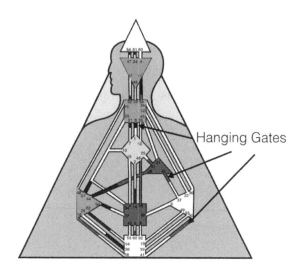

A Hanging Gate is always attracted to people who have the other half of the Channel. This is called electromagnetic attraction.

There are 32 Channels in the Human Design body graph. Each Channel has two halves called Gates. There are a total of 64 Gates. The 64 Gates correlate to the 64 Hexagrams in the Chinese I 'Ching. Each active Gate in your chart adds a different "flavor" to your personality.

You may notice that some of your Gates are colored differently. The black gates are derived from the black numbers on the left of your body graph chart. Gates colored black give you information about your Soul Purpose and of which you are consciously aware. So, for example, if you have Gate 11 coming out of the Ajna Center towards the throat colored black, then you would be consciously aware that you have a lot of ideas!

Some of the gates on your body graph may be colored red. The red gates are derived from the red numbers on the left side of your body graph and give you information about your Life Purpose. Again, for example, if you have Gate 13, The Gate of the Witness being unconscious (red), then you may not be aware that your energy field communicates to others that they are safe to share their secrets with you. You probably have no idea why people are always coming up to you, unexpected, and telling you their deepest, darkest secrets.

If you have checkered Gates, meaning the line to the Gate is in red and black, it means that those energies are part of your Soul and Life Purpose and are often a strong theme in your life. You express those personality aspects both in your conscious and unconscious definition whereas a white line represents an "open" gate. You will always take in the energy of that open Gate from the world around you, and its expression through you will be inconsistent depending on your environment.

When you look at the numbers on the left side of the Body Graph, you will see that each Gate's number has a smaller number next to it. For each Gate, there are six different "lines", that are each line being a further expression of your uniqueness. The lines of the Gates do not show up on the Body Graph, but their meaning can be revealed to you during a Human Design analysis. (You can refer to the traditional Chinese I'Ching to gain more insight into each Gate.)

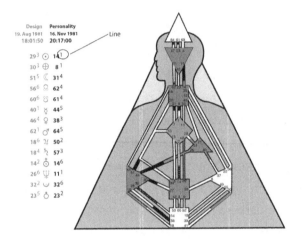

Type

When you look at the bottom of your chart, you will see your type listed. There are five types in the Human Design system. Each type has a specific strategy for making powerful decisions.

The easiest way to begin benefiting from Human Design concepts is to know your Type and to follow the strategy for that type. In the Human Design System, there are five personality "Types." Each has a unique Strategy for making decisions. Knowing your Type can help you develop confidence and trust in your capacity to make reliable decisions for yourself.

The five Types are: the Manifestor, the Manifesting Generator, the Generator, the Projector, and the Reflector. Each Type has a different role to play when interacting with others and the world.

Emotional Theme

Each Human Design Type has an emotional theme, (on some version of a chart also identified as a Life Theme) which is simply part of a person's life and brings them lessons as well as opportunities for growth. When you experience your emotional theme in a strong way, it's usually a sign that you are not living true to yourself. It's always good to take a step back and evaluate your life if you're feeling your emotional theme in a powerful way.

When you live your life according to your Human Design Strategy, you lessen the intensity of your experience with your emotional theme. You might feel it here and there, but it won't be a roaring monster that dogs you day and night. Following your Strategy makes your entire life experience easier and more enjoyable.

The emotional theme is thematic, meaning that you will either be experiencing the emotions of your theme yourself or you may be experiencing them in other people around you who are responding to your behavior.

So, for example, if you are a Manifestor Type, the Manifestor has an emotional theme of anger. A Manifestor has a strategy of needing to inform people before they do things (a hard thing for a Manifestor). It can make a Manifestor feel a little angry that they must inform before they do, but they will experience a lot less anger directed AT them if they inform first.

Strategy

Every Type has a unique way of making decisions and taking action in the world called "Strategy." Your strategy comes from your Type. Strategy is the most important knowledge offered by your Human Design Chart. Your strategy is basically your personal way to make effective decisions. It gives you key information about how to operate your human vehicle in the world, how to make the right choices for you, and how to recognize when you are on the right path in life.

Following your Strategy offers you the opportunity to experience events and circumstances that are correct for you. Not following the Strategy for your Type brings events and experiences into your life that may not be correct for you.

Because learning to follow Strategy effectively can take months or years of practice, you can benefit from coaching by a Human Design Analyst who can provide you with feedback and encouragement.

Follow your Strategy, and you will more naturally align with your Life Purpose, minimize resistance in your life, make strong and healthy decisions that will feel good, more meaningful, and joyful, and you will truly fulfill your Personal Destiny.

Profile

There are twelve different personality "Profiles" in the Human Design system. We derive an individual's profile from the lines of the Gates in his or her conscious and unconscious Sun sign.

The Sun sign is the first sign on a chart under the "Design" and "Personality" columns. The lines are the little numbers just to the right of the big numbers. They look like exponents or a number being raised "to the power of" in mathematics.

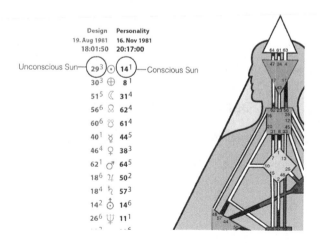

Profiles tell you about major life themes that you will encounter, and they illustrate another way in which your personality interacts with the world. Everyone comes into the world with a specific profile and purpose. Knowing your profile can help you see some of the themes that you will encounter as you move toward fulfilling your purpose.

Each number in a profile has a specific meaning. The first number in your profile is an element of your personality to which you are consciously aware. The second number in the profile may be unconscious and more hidden from you.

The twelve Profiles are derived from the six possible lines of a particular Gate. Each of these six lines represents a different archetype or style of behavior. Your profile can be thought of as an explanation of your conscious and unconscious archetype and the themes associated with that archetype. Most people are aware of their unconscious profile, but because it is unconscious, they do not have a lot of real control over the expression of it. Next, we talk about the Lines, which when combined, make up the Profile.

Definitions of the Lines

Here are basic definitions for each of the six Profile Lines:

Line 1 - The Investigator needs information and feels safe when they have data. (The internet was created for the First Line profiles.)

Line 2 - The Hermit needs alone time to integrate. Second lines need space to feel good and grounded. Others will always find the Hermit when they hide and call them back out into life.

Line 3 - The Experiential Learner needs to experiment with their ideas and to be allowed to "make mistakes" without judgment. There is no getting it "wrong" for the Third line, only figuring out what works based on their understanding of what doesn't work.

Line 4 - The Opportunist builds a foundation of friendships and needs to network as well as share. Fourth Lines need people to accept them for who they are; they need to know what's next and be prepared to feel safe. (Fourth line Profiles don't do "limbo" well.)

Line 5 - The Teacher is here to teach whatever they've experienced in life. They are Karmic Mirrors and are often subject to the projections of others because other people see through their relationships with the Fifth Line profiles what they need to heal the most. Fifth lines need to trust that you will see the truth about them to feel safe and can sometimes hide their truth very deeply when you first get to know them.

Line 6 - The Role Model is the embodiment of what they are here to share with the world. Sixth Lines need to walk their talk. The Sixth line goes through three distinct life phases. The first phase (birth until 30) is a youthful phase of experimentation and experiential learning. The Second phase (30-50) is a long cycle of integration and studying. The final phase (50+) is a cycle of living what they've learned. Sixth lines need to feel that what they are participating in is worth their effort to find meaning and energy in life.

The twelve Profiles listed here are combinations of two of those lines (the "conscious" line followed by the "unconscious" line).

The Twelve Profiles

1/3
Investigator/Experiential Learner

1/4
Investigator/Opportunist

2/4
Hermit/Opportunist

2/5
Hermit/Teacher

3/5
Experiential Learner/Teacher

3/6
Martyr/Role Model

4/6
Opportunist/Role Model

4/1
Opportunist/Investigator

5/1
Teacher/Investigator

5/2
Teacher/Hermit

6/2
Role Model/Hermit

6/3
Role Model/Experiential Learner

Incarnation Cross

The piece of the chart ties the whole thing together is called the Incarnation Cross. The Incarnation Cross is comprised of the energies that make up the Design (Unconscious) and Personality (Conscious) and Sun and Earth

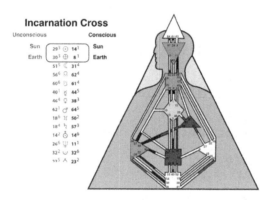

These four energies combined comprise about 70% of the personality expression of a person. The Incarnation Cross in a chart is basically the archetype of a person. It tells us who they are, what they are driven to do, their foibles, follies, and ultimately their destiny if they choose.

There are 192 Incarnation Crosses, each one a reflection of the solar and earth transits. The Incarnation Cross gives us much more information than a mere sun sign in astrology. It offers a deeper explanation for the path of a soul and the journey of a lifetime.

Definition

Definition of the chart refers to the connections between Centers. Single Definition means that all the Centers that are colored in or defined in the chart are all connected.

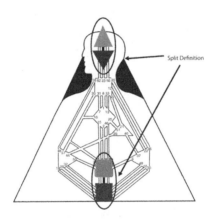

Split Definition means that there are two distinct groups of Energy Centers that are connected within the group but are not connected to each other. Here is an example of a Split Definition below.

Triple Split Definition means that there are three distinct groupings of Energy Centers that are independent yet not connected to each other. Here is an example of a Triple Split Definition below.

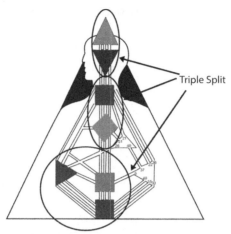

Triple Split

Quadruple Split means that there are four distinct groupings of Energy Centers that are independent and not connected to each other. People with Quadruple Split definition are fairly rare. Here is an example of a Quadruple Split Definition below.

An energy Split can make you feel like you have certain very distinct different aspects to your perception of yourself. For example, in this Quad Split chart, you may feel

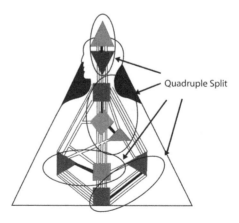

Quadruple Split

like you have a very powerful mind and can get "lost in your head" while you also have an "earthy" and kind of primal part of your personality as well.

In relationships, you are often attracted to partners who have the Gates that "bridge" your splits. When these Gates are defined in a partner, in that particular relationship, you feel "whole" or like all the parts of yourself are unified (which is indeed what happens, at least energetically).

Authority

Authority refers to an aspect of your design that influences your decision-making strategy. Although decision-making is tied directly to your Strategy, your authority flavors the way you use your Strategy.

Authority is determined by certain Centers in your personal Body Graph that will have the most powerful influence on you when you make decisions. Not all Centers carry authority, so your personal authority will depend on your type and your definition.

Authority will also depend on your life conditioning and your level of emotional well-being. When you receive a Human Design Analysis, you are taught to understand patterns of pain and behaviors that may be keeping you from living out the beauty of the mythology of who you really are.

With cognitive awareness of old patterns, you begin to heal and transform these energies into deep sources of wisdom. The more you clear your old energy patterns, the more effectively your natural decision-making skills (your authority) can function. You can then begin to use your Authority along with your Strategy to help you make better decisions for your life.

Your Authority is listed on your chart. The three Authorities that are most important are:

1. **Emotional Authority** - If you have Emotional Authority, it means that you need time to feel your way through your decisions and choices. You have deep, creative energy and you need time to feel if a choice is right for you or not.

2. **Self-Authority** - If you have Self-Authority, it means that you need to talk about your decisions with others for you to get clear about your choices. You don't need advice. You just need a sounding board, someone who will lovingly listen to you while you talk through your decisions.

3. **Splenic Authority** - Splenic Authority means that you have a deep "gut" response to what's the right decision for you and you need to make your decisions in the moment and spontaneously. It is not good for you and maybe even makes you worry more if you think and contemplate your choices. You are spontaneous and can move quickly.

(If you have any other Authority listed on your chart, it won't be as impactful as the three listed above.)

Conclusion

The parts of the chart are each, in and of them-selves, important and give key insights into a personality. Understanding each part and the role it plays in the story in the story of your life helps you put together a bigger pic-ture and deeper understanding of who you truly are.

Remember, each part is a piece of a whole. While we have to "take the chart apart" in order to understand all its key pieces, the real beauty in the chart is in the synthesis of all of the parts. The true story of who you are is revealed when all of the pieces come together.

The next section is designed to give you a practical guide to deepening your awareness of your True Self in or-der to begin embracing what is right about you and your life. My intention is to support you in connecting with your authentic self in a new and empowered way and helping you stay resilient during times of change.

May you fall madly in love with yourself!

HUMAN DESIGN TYPES

What makes a Type a Type?

Each of the five Types has a unique configuration. To understand what makes a Type a Type, you should first understand energy in the chart.

There are four Centers in the Human Design chart that are motors – energy centers. The four motors are the Will Center, the Solar Plexus, the Sacral and the Root Center. As we talk about connecting motors to the throat below, note these connections may not be direct but may connect through other centers.

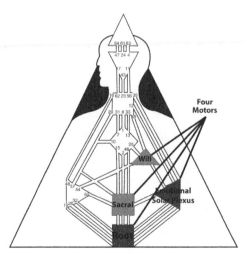

The Sacral Center is the most powerful motor in the body graph and only Generators and Manifesting Generators have a defined (colored) Sacral Center:

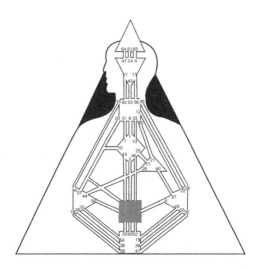

Manifestors: Have an open (white) Sacral Center plus any of the following: a defined Will Center connected via a defined (colored) Channel to the Throat Center, a defined Solar Plexus connected via a defined (colored) Channel to the Throat Center and/or a defined Root Center connected via a defined (colored) Channel to the Throat Center:

Manifesting Generators: Have a defined (colored) Sacral Center plus any of the following: a defined Will Center connected via a defined (colored) Channel to the

Throat Center, and/or a defined Solar Plexus connected via a defined (colored) Channel to the Throat Center and/or a defined Root Center connected via a defined (colored) Channel to the Throat Center and/or a defined (colored) Channel connecting the defined (colored) Sacral Center to the Throat Center.

Generators: Have a defined (colored) Sacral Center and NO motors connected to the Throat Center

Projectors: Have an open (white) Sacral Center and no defined (colored) connections between any of the four motors and the Throat Center.

Reflectors: Have no Centers defined in their charts. Their charts are almost entirely white.

THE MANIFESTOR

FOCUS:

Initiator, Innovative, Empowering, Powerhouse, Provoking

LIFE PURPOSE:

Lead change by initiating others into action

STRATEGY:

Inform those who will be impacted by your actions

EMOTIONAL THEME:

Anger

WEALTH THEME:

Start and leverage something for passive revenue

CHALLENGES:

Lack of sustainable energy, moves faster than others, accessing the right kind of support

PERCENTAGE:

8% Manifestors

ROLE:

Initiate action from ideas and from their own inner creative flow

Manifestors are a minority - around eight percent of all people. If you are a Manifestor, you have an Open Sacral Center and a defined Channel that connects either the Will Center, the Emotional Solar Plexus, or the Root Center to the Throat Center.

You are the only Type designed to initiate action. You are the one who *gets the ball rolling,* the one who makes things happen. All of the other types have to wait before they can take action.

With the sense of knowing right-timing, it's unnecessary for you to wait for outside confirmation before taking action. In spite of this ability to self-initiate, many Manifestors have their own personal way of interacting with the flow of life and wait for signs in their outer world to tell them that the timing is right to act.

Manifestors are powerful creative beings. As a Manifestor, you have an internal, non-verbal creative flow that moves quickly when the timing is correct. This creative flow is so fast that you often don't have time to put words to it. That means when you intuitively sense that the timing is right for you to act, you can just get up and get to it.

Your energy field carries with it the power to initiate others into action. When people are in your energy, they are often unconsciously poised, meaning they are ready to leap and get things going. Because of this frequency of energy, people pay attention to you and are always waiting to see what you do next.

As soon as you take action, other people usually notice and will often interrupt your creative flow. They ask you if you need help or want to know what you're doing. They're not interrupting you because they are trying to stop you. Rather, it's just that they sense that something is about to happen and they feel the need to be a part of it (or to be ready for what's next).

This interruption and these questions can be very difficult for your Manifestor energy. Remember, you have an internal, non-verbal creative flow that you are following. It's an inner, gut-level sense of flow. When you have to stop that flow to find the words to explain to someone what you're doing or that you don't need help, it's often hard to find your creative flow in the same way again. When you don't understand how your energy works, it's easy to react with anger towards other; other people can also become angry with you because they feel that you aren't involving them (or sometimes being considerate of them) when they don't know what you're doing.

As a way of dealing with your energy, others may want to help you. This is their need to feel useful, but it's not your obligation to fulfill this need. You may find that if you are trying to keep others happy to avoid the anger or attempt to control you that you may have often experienced in your life. You may have developed elaborate strategies to secretly do what you want to do without the interference of others. Not being upfront and honest, as hard as it can be, uses up a lot of energy and can make you feel exhausted whenever you feel like you have to deal with people.

The truth is that you could be done with what you're doing in the time it can take to find the right words and try to explain to someone what you're doing. But you'll lose your speed if you don't stop and inform the people around you what you're going to do next.

The trick for you, if you're a Manifestor, is learning to honor your own inner creative flow and letting the people who will be impacted by your actions know what you're doing. Informing is NOT asking permission. You're not here to ask people for permission.

Learning to honor your creative flow, informing others, and not letting other people's discomfort with your choices is often the greatest place of learning for Manifestors.

Common Traps or Challenges

Working regular "9-5 hours" or more is very difficult and unnatural for the Manifestor. As a Manifestor, you need to be very conscious about structuring your business around your energy because you don't have sustainable energy for work.

Manifestors don't usually make good team players and tend to want to do everything themselves. Delegating can be hard for the Manifestor because it feels "faster" to do it yourself; finding the words for your creative flow slows you down and feels unnatural.

Manifestors have a unique energy that makes it easier for them to get things started. Sometimes, when you're a Manifestor, it's easy to lose your patience with other people who simply are not hard-wired the way you are. It can also be difficult, once you get something started, to follow-through with the energy to bring it to completion or to manage your creation on a day to day level. Remember, you're an initiator, not necessarily a "do-er."

Manifestors do NOT have *sustainable* life and work force energy, which is why most are not particularly good at seeing a project or fulfilling an idea to its end. Manifestors are not designed to finish the sustained implementation of ideas and projects. The follow-through and maintenance tasks are not in their Type. Theirs is a creative and initiating energy. They originate opportunities and move on to create the next.

Manifestors give the rest of us reasons to respond— you are like the cue ball on a pool table, bumping into the other balls and causing them to move.

Strategy

If you are a Manifestor, it's correct for you to start things, not necessarily implement the details or finish the projects. You must learn to delegate and/or move on when it feels correct to do so.

If you're feeling stuck or "shut down," start initiating more in your life. It's okay to start with small tasks and projects to rebuild that "initiating muscle." After all, it may have been suppressed for most (or all) of your life.

You'll feel MUCH better when you are behaving the way you are designed to behave. And you'll have more energy...

Remember to inform people who may be impacted by your actions before you act. It takes courage to do this; it will take time for it to become a habit but will be worth it. Your relationships and even your health and wellness will improve because of it. It will also minimize the amount of anger and resistance that you experience from others.

Keep in mind that informing is NOT asking for permission, so don't be afraid of others saying no or trying to stop you. You can still do as intended, but it'll be wise to take other's views into consideration if you can...there's nothing wrong with a second opinion!

Recognize the impact you have on people around you. You have a very strong and powerful aura. Others will usually feel your presence when you enter a room. Some Manifestors are surprised to learn this about themselves, but the people around them know it to be true.

Trust what 'feels' right to you (not just what your brain-based analysis tells you). Manage your energy and take breaks when needed; don't try to keep up with the sustainable energy of Generators and Manifesting Generators. It's MUCH easier to avoid burnout than to recover from it!

Manifestors can initiate action and opportunity without waiting. Manifestors are energy beings that possess tremendous initiating power, but they have to use their power carefully or risk angering others.

Their purpose in life is to create action for a reaction. If a Manifestor decides to start a business, for example, all they have to do is decide on the right timing and then just do it. All of the other types should wait before they can take action. Although most of us think we would love to be Manifestors, being a Manifestor can have its own challenges. Many Manifestors have struggled to learn to use their power appropriately and may be conditioned to hide their power (or suppress it entirely).

Manifestors must learn how to channel their energy properly, or they will face tremendous resistance in life. Properly channeled Manifestor energy often gives the other four Types ideas for projects for responding.

Without informing, you will get resistance every step of the way. That's why many Manifestors (already starting in their childhood) resign after being punished repeatedly by parents, teachers, and others who don't understand the power of the Manifestor.

When Manifestors give up their manifesting powers, they surrender to going through life just getting by. They may feel ignored or like they've been run over by a truck.

The last thing they would want to do is to inform others. Everybody else is in their way all the time, so the idea of making it easier for others by informing is unacceptable. Yet it's the only way out of the circle of control and resistance. (While still living with parents, Manifestors' strategy is actually different - they need to ask for permission.)

Emotional Theme

The emotional theme of Manifestors is anger. Anger often happens when people inadvertently slow you down, try to "help" you or tell you can't do something. Not having the skills to manage anger properly can sometimes be destructive.

Manifestors often struggle with knowing when enough is enough. If you're a Manifestor, it's important to gauge what you're doing and make sure you're not frying everyone else's energy causing them to burn out. If you are, that doesn't mean that you should stop what you're doing, but be aware that sometimes this may trigger anger in others.

On an energy level, you have quite the impression on others, but your aura doesn't communicate as much as the auras of other types. Because of this, others are not sure how to accept you, which is why communication is so important. Inform those in your circle of influence. This is how to release the tension others may feel about you. By bringing them into the conversation, they may help you and put their energy into whatever it is that you have initiated. At that point, you will find what you've been seeking, completion of your creative inspiration.

Relationships

If You LOVE a Manifestor, see that you don't take their anger personally; understand that it's part of their process.

Accept that they may not "need" you in the way you need them and that it's nothing against you. They are designed to act on their own, but they can engage and inspire people when "in tune" with those around them, particularly when keeping them informed of their dreams and plans.

Don't interrupt them when they're in their "groove" of figuring things out and getting things done. They're not ignoring you—they are simply completely engaged in their own internal process.

Keep them informed about YOUR actions, and make it easy for them to inform you… without fear of recrimination or rejection.

Respect their privacy; don't ask or pry. They may not always be able to articulate what's going on their mind.

Trust them in their role of initiating action and giving others things to which they may respond—that's what they're here to do!

Don't judge or criticize when they start then stop projects. Trying is often the only way they can know if something is correct for them. Instead, allow them their own consequences—they usually don't want to be "helped" unless they've asked for help.

Manifestor Children

One of the hardest things to do when you are a parent of a Manifestor is to let them go and to allow them to discover their own inner creative flow. It's ironic that most parents of Manifestors want to hold them back. This isn't because as the parent of a Manifestor that you want to control or harm your child. It's just that the aura of a Manifestor energetically sends the message that this is a child who follows a different set of rules, who isn't necessarily going to follow the rules, and who is often quite proficient, effective, and taking care of themselves.

Here are a few things that Manifestor children need:

- The freedom to follow their creative input.
- To be informed and to learn to inform.
- Downtime and regular rest.
- To learn when enough is enough.

The natural response of parents is to want to hold tight, keep this creative force from going out into the world and getting hurt, or stop the child from taking big risks. The challenge for parents of Manifestors is learning to trust your child's inner creative instincts and wisdom while helping your child to grow as well as thrive.

Manifestor children need a lot of freedom to experiment and explore. In addition, they also need downtime, often away from others, to restore and nourish their own energy. They also need to be carefully informed about plans and what to expect so that they can flow along with the rest of the family.

Work

The design of Manifestors can very much affect relationships as well as work and life choices.

Manifestors CAN and DO have jobs or businesses and raise families, but they may burnout around age 50 (or before) if they continue attempting to accomplish too much, especially if pushing themselves to keep up with the 70% of the population who do have consistent Sacral energy.

Manifestors don't "need" people the way other Types need people, which affects how they operate within relationships. The biggest challenge (and a key piece of their Strategy for success in life) is INFORMING those who are affected by their actions before acting.

More so than other Types, Manifestors don't like being told what to do. If they feel obligated to ask permission to do something or feel manipulated in any way, they may become overtly defiant and angry towards or feel repressed by others, turning those feelings inward and creating anxiety, depression, or even illness.

Health

For Manifestors to stay healthy, they need to be powerful. If you have not been using your power, or if you've shut yourself off from your Manifestor energy, your energy doesn't go away. It ricochets inside in your body either burning you out, sometimes creating depression and anxiety.

If you have a lifetime of using your power without informing others, if you have fought and struggled to keep people out of your way so that you can do what you feel like you need to do, then you may also experience burnout.

Most Manifestors burn out around the age of 50 if they haven't been using their energy properly. Burnout can come from not knowing when enough is enough, pushing without the balance of rest, trying to work in ways that are not in alignment with your energy, and denying your own power. If you're burned out, the number one priority in your life is healing the burnout. Often that means stopping everything in your life and catching up on the rest you need to restore and recharge your energy and your body.

Getting good healthy sleep is of particular importance for Manifestors, and to do so, you need to lie down before you feel tired. You can read or watch a movie for a while before you fall asleep, but lying in a horizontal position. Being flat in a horizontal position allows you to release the energy that you've taken in during the day and helps your body discharge excess energy.

If possible, sleep alone, not in range of other people's aura. If you can do this, you will feel the difference in the morning. If you share a house or live in an apartment, remember that there may be a neighbor above or behind the wall where you are sleeping. If you're closer than your two arm-lengths, you are still in each other's aura. You'll sleep better if you can reposition your bed to be as far away from the energy of others as possible.

Wealth

Passive revenue streams or ways of making money via investments versus labor are important for Manifestors. If you are a young Manifestor, start early saving and investing your money.

Spiritual Themes

Manifestors have powerful auras and have an energetic impact on those around them. That impact can be positive and pull people in, or it can repel people.

They have a much easier time of "making things happen" in the world than any of the other Types, if they are living true to their Type.

The Manifestor is tuned into the flow of creation in the world. They are energetic messengers, designed to take actions that initiation a flow of Divine Inspiration on the planet.

If you're a Manifestor, you have a powerful role in changing the world. You may have, at various times in your life, wondered if you had a purpose or a reason to be here. The more connected you are to your own spiritual practice, the more aligned you will feel with the purpose and the greater service you will offer the world - in the way that's right for you.

Some famous Manifestors include Al Gore, George W. Bush, Jack Nicholson, Susan Sarandon and Richard Burton, Vladamir Putin.

THE DETAILS OF DESIGN

MANIFESTOR

AT A GLANCE

Initiate Action & Get Started

Focus:

Initiator
Powerhouse • Empowering
Innovative • Provoking

Supportive Actions:

- ♥ Moving fast (decisions, action) is your natural speed

- ♥ Inform, or risk anger

- ♥ Know when enough is enough

- ♥ Rest to avoid burnout

- ♥ Use your power to stay healthy

- ♥ Create passive income streams

- ♥ Relax before sleep

Challenges:

- ♠* Working 9-5 is unnatural

- ♠* Being a team player

- ♠* Recognizing impact on others

THE GENERATOR AND THE MANIFESTING GENERATOR

There are two types of Generators: Pure Generators and Manifesting Generators. About 70% of us are Generators (either of these two Types). Pure and Manifesting Generators have defined Sacral Centers that allow them the gift to create the *work of the world.*

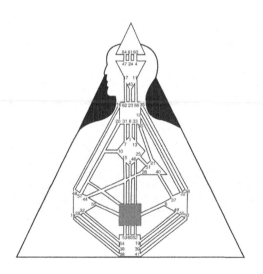

THE GENERATOR

FOCUS:

Respond, Right Work, Family, Mastery, Here to Build

LIFE PURPOSE:

Build (work, family)

STRATEGY:

Respond, then act

EMOTIONAL THEME:

Frustration

WEALTH THEME:

Mastery over time

CHALLENGES:

Finding right work, frustration and quitting, patience and waiting, trusting their inner response (Sacral)

PERCENTAGE:

35% Generators

ROLE:

To do the work of the world and to find mastery in their work

Generators play the part of patient seekers who become fully activated in their life purpose when they learn to respond to what the world brings them instead of trying to "figure out" with their minds what they should be doing. The Generators have the potential to be Masters of what they respond to do and to create.

Generators know they hold this energy. If you're a Generator Type, you often feel frustrated because you can sense deep inside of yourself that you're here to do something that fulfills your full potential. As a Generator, you're trained by the world to use your thinking and the power of your mind to set your path to mastery. The truth for Generators is that the path is revealed to you by the world outside of yourself; it takes faith and the understanding of how to connect with that path correctly to align yourself with your destiny and the ultimate fulfillment of your potential.

In other words, if you're a Generator Type, you can't simply follow your ideas. You have to wait for something outside of yourself to confirm that:

- Your idea IS actually the right idea for you.
- The timing is now right to take action on your idea.

Strategy

The Generator Strategy is to wait to respond. This is a simple, although often confusing aspect for the Generator. "Wait to respond" simply means that even if you have an incredibly inspiring insight, thought, or idea, you need to wait for confirmation in your outer world before you take action.

Confirmation in your outside world can be someone saying something to you, a "sign" from the Universe, or some kind of physical initiation that comes from outside of your mind. Once you get the "sign" or something to which you know you should respond, as a Generator Type, you can then act on the inspirations that feel good and right.

As a Generator, in order to find your path, you have to learn how to use your energy correctly. Generator Types are the only Types who have a defined Sacral Motor. The Sacral Motor is the source of a direction-giving, non-verbal, gut-level vibration that tells you what feels right and what doesn't.

You may experience the Sacral response as a "gut feeling", and you can connect with it even more deeply when you express that gut-feeling with a non-verbal sound. The "Sacral Sound" sounds like "uh-huh" for a "yes" and "un-uhn" for a "no." Most Generators naturally make these sounds, but are often taught that they are rude or to "use our words instead." When you watch Generator children, you'll notice that they are grunting, humming, sound-based beings. When you lose touch with the power of these sounds, you lose touch with your special inner compass that is designed to signal you to show you which direction is yours to follow.

This Sacral Sound is the sound of your inner intuition, the vibrational alignment with your correct direction in life. It is that direction that will take you to the next step in the unfolding of your mastery. The Sacral is truth; it cannot lie.

The Sacral Center is a source of sustainable energy. All of the motors in the Human Design System, except for the Sacral, have wave-like, inconsistent qualities, but the Sacral keeps going and going. It is energy for work and life force. It's about providing the resources, education, children, taking care of the family, the tribe, and the community. It's about work in every way and doing it all sustainably.

Generators have *two* primary focuses in life: work and family. As a Generator, you will feel most fulfilled when you are pursuing either of these two focuses or both.

For Generators, life is about RESPONSE. Instead of chasing after an imitation life, Generators must be patient and allow an authentic life to appear. The goal of a Generator is to discover, pursue, and dedicate their life to what they love.

Common Traps and Challenges

Most Generators have been taught to bypass their own inner wisdom and to adopt a *"just do it"* attitude about the things they think they "should" be doing. Generators may find it difficult to refrain from "just doing it" because it requires ignoring old programming and old ideas about hard work, success, and money. It can feel scary or irresponsible to follow your gut (your inner wisdom) and forego the programming of your mind.

Because Generators are energy beings, they have the energy to work, even at jobs they hate. Sadly, many Generators do this for their entire lives. When a Generator is simply working, but not working at a job they responded to, they fail to tap into the full expression of their potential and the vital Life Force energy that turns on when they respond to doing the work that feels right. When a Generator responds in the manner of haste, then frustration and burnout eventually ensue. It's not until Generators are patient and withhold pursuing what they "think" they should be doing and let their life path unfold in front of them that the energy appears. In essence, it's like waiting for a "sign" or a signal that the timing must be right before acting.

When a Generator waits, they create a magical force that attracts everyone to them. When a Generator waits, others come over and ask them. When a Generator waits, they create an energy that will continue to grow until a true purpose appears.

Every Generator has a fear that if they do nothing, then no one will ask them anything. But every Generator who has the courage to wait, soon sees that fear is unfounded.

When a Generator waits and steps into their full purpose and potential, they wake up to the vitality and a joy that they've been waiting for their whole lives.

Emotional Theme

The uh-huh and the un-unh turn on the Sacral Motor. That's your truth. The gut feelings are for the Generators. The "gut" is the source of the truth. You must ask questions of yourself and monitor your gut response with the uh-huh and un-unh. When you aren't responding, you will most likely experience frustration.

The Sacral is a tremendous energy generator that provides *all energy*. Sacral energy is enough to do all things when you follow that gut pulse. Generators who don't respond to the energy end up deeply frustrated. It's imperative to remain patient and recognize the presence of the energy when it appears. The power of the defined Sacral Center will lead the way to one's true life purpose. Trust your inner response (Sacral). The Sacral Center provides Generators with a virtually inexhaustible source of energy.

Generators can find themselves being confined to work they hate, feeling the drudgery of routine without joy, lost in unproductive labor, feeling there is something missing, knowing they may have made a mistake—and not knowing how to get out of it unless they quit. Ultimately, they will burn out or live life at a level of compromise, which will create more and more frustration, or simply have a life of quiet despair.

There is a second source of natural frustration for the Generator, too. Generators have a "stair-step" learning curve. It is normal that once a Generator responds to a new opportunity that there will be a surge in mastery. It feels good to be doing or learning something new, and Generators can learn quickly. But, eventually, all Generators hit a plateau. It can feel like you're "stuck" and that nothing is happening.

Being on plateaus is normal for Generators, and it is a phase of learning, energy integration, and growth. The plateau can be dangerous for the Generator who doesn't understand their unique energy. The tendency for many Generators is to quit when they are on the plateau, failing to recognize that the plateau is simply a normal part of the Generator process.

When you understand that it is crucial to wait for the next thing to respond to when you are on the plateau, you are present then ready when the next step to your growth and mastery shows up. Frustration is simply a sign that you are getting ready for something new.

But, if you quit instead of wait, as many Generators do, you may miss the next true opportunity for your growth and mastery. Instead, you spend a lifetime of starting and quitting and starting and quitting, never getting to be masterful at what you are really created to do.

Relationships

Trust your relationship with a Generator. Allow the Generator the time to wait for things that will prompt a response; the Generator also needs the freedom to honor and follow their responses... even if their responses "appear" to not be logical.

The most respectful—and helpful—way that you can interact with a Generator is to ask them Yes/No questions. This allows them a clear opportunity for their Sacral Center to respond and give them guidance.

Don't take their frustration/anger/impatience personally. Recognize that it's part of their process, and when you support them in being true to their Generator nature, you'll help them minimize all of the things that are distractions to them and confusing to you. Understand that it is correct for them to wait for their inner guidance before they take action.

Once this energy difference in your relationship is truly understood and respected, you'll both be happier. Most of all, enjoy the ride!

Generator Children

Generator children need to learn about their own inner compass and their Sacral energy. It is vital for Generator children to learn to respond. Yes/No question games that help them respond with the Sacral sounds are fun, enlivening and vital to helping Generator children stay connected to their own inner truth. They need to

- Explore & engage in activities.
- Learn in a self-paced environment.
- Engage in daily exercise and physical activity.

Generator children need to move and groove. They need a lot of physical activity to wear them out and promote good sleep every day. Too much time sitting and lack of movement can cause Generator children to have challenges with sleep and even health. Turn off the computers, don't overdo the homework and after-school activities and help your Generator child get moving. Your whole family will benefit!!

Work

Generators are the great *Workers of the World.* They are often performing relentless work they hate, tolerating a lifetime of labor while waiting for the sacral energy to reveal their life's goal.

The one true purpose is for Generators to be patient, to trust their tremendous energy and power to fulfill their purpose of not only finding, but also becoming masterful at their "right work." When Generators are doing their "right work" - the work that feels satisfying and juicy - then they not only feel good, they are adding to the wholeness and abundance of the world.

SATISFACTION is a keyword for Generators; it's all about tapping into sacral energies that open the door to the satisfaction of *work and family*. Your Sacral response will take you to where you can experience the greatest satisfaction, vitality, and joy.

Health

Your brain will often work hard to figure out the right answers, but that is NOT where YOU want to be making your decisions and choices. That's what your Sacral responses are intended to do. Generators who have not tuned into their Sacral motor for a lifetime are vulnerable to burnout. Not being true to your energy and trying to do something that doesn't satisfy you can make you exhausted.

Here are some ways that Generators can lose energy or burnout:

- Not loving work or environment.
- Sedentary lifestyle.
- Not following their Sacral guidance.
- Over-exerting themselves & not recharging their energy.
- Feeling frustrated and impatient when results aren't quickly realized

Generators have their own inner guidance system (Sacral) that can tell them what they need to do for health and wellness. They need to respond to what's healthy. It has to feel right and aligned with their Sacral to commit to a health and wellness routine.

As energy beings, Generators need a lot of movement and exercise to burn off excess energy. Generators who are struggling with insomnia or poor-quality sleep can benefit from more physical activity.

Wealth

The wealth theme of the Generator is to become masterful at whatever makes them respond. But, for Generators, recognizing when to respond and when to remain dormant is their greatest challenge.

Most Generators get frustrated when they hit their plateau of inertia and many quit before they surge in mastery; this denies them the blessing and opportunity of experiencing whatever it is they are here to *build in the world*. To align with true abundance, the Generators must learn to wait and manage frustration in healthy and dynamic ways so to be ready to master life's purpose.

The Generator Types can work to make money and even work hard to make money provided that the work they are doing is work that to which they have responded positively with their Sacral motors. The more they love their work and their masterful contribution, the easier it becomes for them to create and maintain wealth. Frustrated and burned out Generators can often overspend their funds as a way of overcompensating for their frustration.

Patience and passion are the keys to building true wealth for the Generator.

Spiritual Themes

A Generator will wait to respond in a world that's been taught to pursue arbitrary opportunities. By this nature, it's imperative that Generators be patient and wait to see what the Universe delivers to them. Only then, when the right thing shows up - the thing that *feels* right - follow that feeling, respond, and take right action.

The goal of the Generator is to achieve mastery. Generators cannot achieve mastery if they're leaping into things that don't feel right because they are afraid to trust in the natural unfolding of their life and the abundance of the Universe.

It is the Generator's job to take inspiration and give it form through creative work. The Generators build the manifested form of Cosmic Order, and when they follow their Sacral impulses, they are led to their right place and their right destiny in the world.

The spiritual challenge of the Generator is to trust the unfolding of Divine Order and their place in it by trusting the inner wisdom of their Sacral impulse.

Famous Pure Generators: Albert Einstein, Dalai Lama, Elvis Presley, Bill Clinton, Meryl Streep, John

Lennon, Madonna, James Dean, Vladimir Lenin, Carl Jung, Timothy Leary, Oprah Winfrey, Meg Ryan, Greta Garbo, Margaret Thatcher, Deepak Chopra, Jay Z, Kim Kardashian.

THE DETAILS OF DESIGN

GENERATOR

AT A GLANCE

Respond to Life

Focus:

Mastery
Respond • Right Work • Family
Here to Build

Supportive Actions:

- ♥ Mastery through repetition over time
- ♥ Create in response to life
- ♥ Know when to quit
- ♥ Use your mind to visualize (use your gut to decide)
- ♥ Move your energy physically to avoid frustration
- ♥ Wear yourself out every day for good sleep
- ♥ Cultivate a practice of patience

Challenges:

- ☀ Quitting out of frustration
- ☀ Trying to manifest your thoughts
- ☀ Feeling stuck

THE MANIFESTING GENERATOR

FOCUS:

Shortcuts to Mastery, Respond, Right Work, Family, Here to Build

LIFE PURPOSE:

Build (work, family)

STRATEGY:

Respond, then envision, inform, then act

EMOTIONAL THEME:

Frustration and anger

WEALTH THEME:

Mastery over time

CHALLENGES:

Finding right work, frustration and quitting, patience and waiting, trusting their inner response (Sacral)

PERCENTAGE:

35% Manifesting Generators

ROLE:

To do the work of the world and to find mastery in their work.

(**If you are a Manifesting Generator, you are a hybrid of both the Manifestor and the Generator, although you are still a "Generator Type." Please read the Manifestor section along with the Generator section to get more insights into how you operate.)

Considered the most powerful motor in the body, the Sacral is the Center that controls *work and life force energy*, therefore gifting Manifesting Generators with the ability to multi-task work and family.

Manifesting Generators have a deep inner awareness to know what's right for them as they wait for a "sign" or a signal that the timing is right to act. A strong intuition turned on by gut-level pulses will simultaneously place Manifesting Generators in the right place, doing the right work, having the right impact.

Common Traps or Challenges

What makes a Manifesting Generator? Let's get right to the point. If you are an MG, you want to read these bullets.

- A Defined Sacral Center, the most powerful motor in the body, focuses work and life force energy.
- A motorized energy connects through a channel to the throat. That means Manifesting Generators can initiate conversations, although still

need to act like Generators in other areas of their lives. (They need to wait to respond.)

- Finding the right work and right partner in life is important, and finding the fastest way to do them is the way a Manifesting Generator will approach these topics.
- Patience is extremely important and waiting to respond with Sacral energy as well as informing everyone in your "impact field" before you act needs to be top-of-mind.

Manifesting Generators determine the fastest way to complete tasks, often skipping steps in the process while getting things "done." If they find those skipped steps to be important, they will eventually complete them.

Manifesting Generators are the busiest Type. They are intense multi-taskers, filled with enormous bursts of energy who feel nothing seems to move fast enough. When fatigue comes, they will take the time to recharge, only to start all over again.

Strategy

Manifesting Generators have two primary focuses in life: work and family. One, or both, may be the primary focus.

Manifesting Generators are multi-taskers, oftentimes *serial entrepreneurs*. They need and love to do more than one thing at a time. They often speed through creating anything and everything they consider.

Manifesting Generators are designed to discover the shortcut—the fastest, easiest way to getting things done. Once they begin a project, Manifesting Generators will have best results when including family, team, staff, or peers as they, too, will be affected by the actions. However, Manifesting Generators (much like the Manifestor) have to inform these groups about the actions prior to following through.

Manifesting Generators (and Generators) recognize that the most important thing in life is finding the *right work*. If a Manifesting Generator isn't working on something they love, burnout occurs; if satisfaction isn't found, frustration and unhappiness take hold. In contrast, when they realize their *true* work, Sacral Center provides them a virtually inexhaustible source of energy.

Manifesting Generators respond quite quickly to situations because of the motor to the Throat, so it's difficult to tell the difference between responding and initiating. Once a response is made, the Manifesting Generator *should* stop and envision their next decision. *They will do well if ideas are imagined first for a visualized outcome before actually doing.* However, they must still wait before taking action.

It is normal and healthy for Manifesting Generators to be starting many projects at the same time. They do not have to complete these projects but instead need to follow the flow of the projects that feel good as they are unfolding in a satisfying way.

This process of trying many things simultaneously often causes others to judge the Manifesting Generator for over-committing or lack of focus, but this is actually an important part of the creative process of the Manifesting Generator. They need to be free to try many things at once.

Emotional Theme

Manifesting Generators experience deep frustration by initiating (starting) things. For example, years ago I had an idea for a workshop, after organizing and marketing it like crazy, the sales for the workshop were almost nonexistent! Talk about frustrating! Afterwards, I started studying Human Design. I waited and waited (ugh) until someone suggested I *teach* a workshop. I responded to that request, and the workshop sold out!

Of course, waiting can feel very challenging. It may feel unnatural for us, particularly in our culture as we are told *get out there and just do it*. Make something happen. If you're a Manifesting Generator, experiment with waiting—try it if just a few days. See what happens!

Your energy field communicates to the world that you need something that will enable you to respond to it. When Manifesting Generators wait, things always come to them *at the right time and the right way*. Manifesting Generators have similar energy characteristics as Manifestors, though tend to respond more quickly to situations than a pure Generator.

It may seem that Manifesting Generators continually change their minds. For them, the need to internally check responses by trial and error as they respond to situations confirms (or not) if what they've started is "still good for them." In essence, it's like waiting for a "sign" or a signal that the timing is right before taking action. Manifesting Generators have an awareness if something is right or wrong for them. They have a *gut instinct* that, when followed correctly, always puts them in the *right place at the right time.*

A Manifesting Generator is uniquely capable of getting more accomplished than most, and for a longer period of time. For those who don't respond, they run the risk of being very busy accomplishing nothing.

The emotional themes of the Manifesting Generator are anger and frustration. That is why the emotional theme of the Manifesting Generator is anger (from the Manifesting part of the personality) and frustration (from the Generator part of the personality). Manifesting Generators must also inform like Manifestors in order to stabilize the energy around them. They can go so fast that informing feels like it is slowing them down, but informing will decrease the resistance they get from others.

Like Pure Generators, they tend to sit on plateaus before they have breakthroughs. It's common for Manifesting Generators to quit and go a different direction right before the breakthrough. Part of this is attributable to finding work they love. If they don't love their work, it's hard to get it done. If you're feeling stuck and you're a Manifesting Generator, it might be good to see if you really love what you're doing to make sure your head didn't talk you into something you hate because you think it's profitable. As a Manifesting Generator, your passion is the most profitable part of your business. No passion = no profit.

Sometimes Manifesting Generators get out of balance. They love their work so much they forget to come up for air. Manifesting Generators move very fast, and like Manifestors, often have a hard time with being team players, preferring to work on their own. Delegating and letting go can be challenging; they often need help "triaging" their time as well as energy and making sure they're not doing everything just because they can.

Relationships

Manifesting Generators who use their inherent energy correctly and follow the inner guidance of their Sacral response are a dynamic and powerful force! They benefit the world in work and relationships—and are magnificent to watch in action!

Manifesting Generators can be committed and steady partners in the right relationships. However, they are steadfast, and when *in a groove*, they prefer to be left alone - a problem for relationships! Sometimes when Manifesting Generators are in partnership, they can "steamroll" their partners and peers by virtue of their speed as well as focus on getting the job done.

In addition, all Manifesting Generators will forget occasionally to inform their partners about projects, leaving their partners confused, angry, or even stressed about what might be going on in the relationship. The outer frenetic appearance of the Manifesting Generator creativity can sometimes leave their loved ones feeling overwhelmed by their energy. Informing can help soften the intensity but the creative spark combined with the sustainability of the Sacral energy can feel like it's too much at various times.

As a Manifesting Generator, if you're not waiting for life to "come to you" and responding to it (so you know if you should pursue or not), you won't know what is truly "right" so that you may apply your considerable energy and competence. Have you been rushing off in scattered directions without waiting to respond? The problem with that approach is that's just not correct for you. Hence, you will experience many "wrong" directions, accompanied by frustration, anger, and impatience.

Sadly, closest relationships often bear the brunt of those types of reactions. When you wait and follow your inner guidance, you'll have less frustration spilling onto others. Recognizing that the frustration and anger are energy will help minimize the negative impact on others. However, frustration IS part of your personal learning curve, so you won't be avoiding it entirely. It takes courage to wait for, trust, and follow your Sacral Response...but everything in your life (including relationships) will benefit when you do.

You'll be more effective in your relationships when you work at being as respectful of others as you can, watch out for power struggles, and learn to compromise. Also, remember to INFORM those who will be impacted by your actions BEFORE you take those actions. Don't worry about skipping steps, moving fast, and multi-tasking—you are designed for these! Be physically active during the day so that you are tired when going to bed. You'll wake up each morning with another *full tank of gas*, to be used while doing it all over again. The key to sleeping well is physical activity. This is especially true for Manifesting Generator children, many of whom are incorrectly diagnosed with ADD or ADHD.

If you are not a Manifesting Generator, but are in a relationship with one, follow these guidelines:

- Accept that they move fast, fast, fast, and may leave you behind at times. Don't try to keep up--you will wear down and burnout. Once this energy difference in your relationship is truly understood and respected, you'll both be happier. Most of all, enjoy the ride!

- Understand that it is correct for them to wait for their inner guidance before they act.
- Allow the Manifesting Generator the time to wait for things to which he or she can respond; there needs to be an understanding by the Manifesting Generator to have the freedom to honor and follow their responses... even if their responses "appear" to not be logical.
- The most respectful (and helpful) way that you can interact with a Manifesting Generator is to ask them Yes/No questions. This allows them a clear opportunity for their Sacral Center to respond and give them guidance.
- Don't take their frustration/anger/impatience personally. Recognize that it's part of their process, and when you support them in being true to their Manifesting Generator nature, you'll help them minimize all of that.

Manifesting Generator Children

Just like the Generator child, the Manifesting Generator child needs to be given options and choices in "yes/no" format, such as: "Do you want to wear your green shirt? Or do you like the blue shirt better?"

The more you allow Manifesting Generator children the freedom to choose, the more they stay connected with their inner authority and their inner compass that takes them to the right place (and opportunities) in life. A Manifesting Generator child needs to:

- explore and engage in activities that spark their interest and passion.
- learn in a self- paced environment.
- engage in daily exercise and physical activity.
- rest or go to bed when they are tired and not at a set time.
- be asked, "Do you want to do this?" "Does this feel good to you?" "Is this good for you at this time?" "Is it better for you to do this later?" and "I have a suggestion, do you want to hear it?"

Manifesting Generators may seem to start things and not finish. While you want to encourage children to work towards mastering a skill set or an experience, it's also important for your Manifesting Generator to be allowed to try things and see how they feel before they commit to doing them.

Manifesting Generators often have a low tolerance for frustration and can seem to skip from thing to thing to thing. It's important that you help them learn to connect with their Sacral sounds and stay tuned to the choices that are correct. Make sure that they don't quit unless they respond to quitting. Teach them ways to manage their overwhelming sensation and frustration; give them responsibility for figuring out how to be more masterful. (As a parent, sometimes it feels easier just to take over for your child or resolve the frustrating circumstances. If you do this, you rob your Manifesting Generator of important learning experiences.)

Work

Your brain will often work hard to figure out the right answers for you, but that is NOT where YOU want to be making your decisions and choices—you need to use your Sacral responses. Manifesting Generators have to wait for something to which he or she can respond before they leap into action. This is like waiting for a "sign" or a signal that the timing is right before acting.

Manifesting Generators have a deep inner awareness that "pulses" on or off. Following these strong gut-level pulses puts the Manifesting Generator *in the right place, doing the right work, and having the right impact.* In addition, Manifesting Generators have a unique ability to multi-task A Manifesting Generator is uniquely capable of getting more things done than most and for a long period of time.

The Manifesting Generator brain will often work hard to figure out the right answers, but that is NOT where YOU want to be making your decisions and choices. That's where your Sacral responses are purposeful. Compared to the pure Generator, who has a much more deliberate process, if the two Types begin a job at the same time, it will appear like the Manifesting Generator is faster and learns more quickly. However, six months later the Generator will have caught up, and they will both be at the same level of mastery.

Health

Manifesting Generators also have sustainable life force and work force energy for doing. Like Generators, they are designed to start with a "full tank of gas" every morning and use up that energy before they go to bed. They are also designed to be fast processors (the fastest of the five Types), have a lot going on, and are good multi-taskers. They may skip steps in their speed to get things done, and that's actually correct for them.

Although their energy is fast and sustainable, it is not inexhaustible (even though they often think they are inexhaustible!). Here are some ways that Manifesting Generators can lose energy or burnout. They will experience a variety of "complications" that will wear down their energy.

- Not loving work or environment
- Sedentary lifestyles
- Not following their Sacral guidance
- Over-exerting themselves & not recharging their energy
- Feeling frustrated, angry & impatient when results aren't seeming

Wealth

Just like the Generator who has a goal of achieving mastery, the Manifesting Generator cannot achieve mastery if they're leaping from thing to thing out of frustration.

The Sacral the Manifesting Generator's truth; it cannot lie, and is turned on by two sounds: *uh-huh and un-unh.* When these sounds are emitted, the Sacral can find its truth. The Sacral is far away from the head, so when operating out of the rudimentary life force energy, if you find yourself having to stop to use words, you're talking out of your head, and this means your energy is far away from your Sacral—that's not good for a Manifesting Generator.

Sacral is your compass, a navigational tool for life. It guides you to where you need to go, when to need to do something, what needs to be accomplished. It's life force energy. That's your truth. When you focus on mastering these concepts, wealth follows.

Spiritual Themes

The Spiritual role of the Manifesting Generator is to shorten the amount of time from thought form to creation. Manifesting Generators are here to remind us that creation can happen instantaneously if we remove our limitations and stay aligned with the unfolding of the Divine Plan.

As our perception of time is evolving, the Manifesting Generators have their own unique way of bending and using time. Watch the Manifesting Generators in your life, and you'll be witnessing new ways to use time and flow.

Some famous Manifesting Generators are: Frederic Chopin, Marie Curie, Hillary Clinton, Clint Eastwood, Sigmund Freud, Mahatma Gandhi, Steffi Graf, Marie Antoinette, Mikhail Gorbachev, Jimi Hendrix, Pope John Paul II, Janis Joplin, Friedrich Nietzsche, Richard Nixon, Yoko Ono, Prince, Jacqueline Onassis, Martin Luther King, Vincent Van Gogh, Malala Yousafzai, Nicki Minaj.

THE DETAILS OF DESIGN

MANIFESTING GENERATOR

AT A GLANCE

Respond by Initiating Action

Focus:
Shortcuts to Mastery
Respond • Right Work • Family
Here to Build

Supportive Actions:

♥ Mastery through repetition and multitasking

♥ Create in response to life

♥ Know when to skip steps

♥ Use your mind to visualize (use your gut to decide)

♥ Move your energy physically to avoid frustration and anger

♥ Wear yourself out every day for good sleep

♥ Cultivate a practice of patience

Challenges:

💣 Quitting out of frustration
💣 Being patient with others
💣 Feeling stuck

THE PROJECTOR

FOCUS

Guidance, Wisdom, Intuitive, Sensitive, Sharing

LIFE PURPOSE

Manage others

STRATEGY:

Wait to be invited

EMOTIONAL THEME:

Bitterness

WEALTH THEME:

Self- mastery upon receiving invitation

CHALLENGES:

Waiting to receive the right invitation,
giving away intellectual property

PERCENTAGE:

24% Projectors

ROLE:

Manage and guide and direct others.

If you are a Projector, you are not here to work. You are here to know others, to recognize them, to direct and guide them. But that can only happen if you yourself are 1) recognized and 2) invited to do so.

Projectors can become the natural managers and leaders of the world. Projectors do not carry energy in their own personal energy field, but absorb the energies of others and manage it. Projectors have to wait to be recognized and invited into the major events in life, such as love relationships, career and right place (where they live).

Common Traps or Challenges

The biggest challenge for Projectors is energy. Projectors don't have a lot of sustainable energy for working in the traditional way we think of as "work". They need to structure their business in a way that allows for significant cycles of rest and restoration.

Because hard work doesn't serve the Projector's purpose, learning how to leverage knowledge is important.

Projectors have a deep energy need for recognition. They often compromise their value for being "seen" and recognized. To many Projectors, being "seen" and recognized, even if it's for the "wrong" thing feels better than waiting for people to notice the value that they carry.

Projectors must value themselves enough to structure their business to be paid for their ideas, insights, and consulting. It's easy for the Projector to give their intellectual property away- *for free.*

Projectors struggle with being heard or having ideas stolen. It's counterintuitive, but learning to wait until someone asks is often the most profitable strategy for the Projector. It makes for an interesting way to do business and life.

When things don't go as planned or the recognition feels slow in coming, the Projector can experience bitterness. Managing the bitterness is crucial as, if it is not kept in check, it can repel people instead of attracting them. This takes a lot of self-mastery, patience, and trust in the abundance of the Universe.

If an invitation feels good for a Projector and is accepted, an enormous amount of energy and power is channeled into that situation, which may be used to manage others and all the world. The challenge for the Projector is to trust that the right invitations will come to them and to wait for those invitations. Sometimes Projectors wait months or years for the right invitation.

Projectors, for all their wisdom, can have a frustrating and debilitating life process if *they* try to push themselves to initiate action. A Projector simply does not have the energy to "just do it;" if they try to initiate like a Manifestor or work steadily like a Generator, they will burn themselves out very quickly.

Because they are "non-energy" types and they are not here to work steadily like the Generator Types, the Projector Types may receive a lot of judgment from others. They may be perceived as "lazy" when, in fact, it is literally unhealthy for these Types to initiate any kind of action or to work at the wrong kind of jobs on a steady basis. They usually can't sustain the energy flow on their own.

Projectors are here to deeply understand others. Projectors can be powerful resources if they are recognized and used properly. A Projector can, simply by watching another energy Type, intuitively know how that other person can maximize their energy and their potential. This makes them natural coaches and mentors. Projectors are here to be recognized and invited by others.

Strategy

If you're a Protector, your strategy is to wait for an invitation to the important areas of life (relationships, work, et cetera). If your authority says yes, then you can really share your gifts and guidance. To be invited means that you are seen and recognized for your values. If you don't wait for an invitation or the energy of invitation, you meet resistance.

Through your open centers, you take others in deeply. You take in other people's definition, and you clearly see who they are. Your aura focuses on the very core of their being, and you recognize others. But if you try to guide others without being invited to do so, you meet resistance, or feel that no one really sees you; no one recognizes you.

Out of that comes a deep feeling of bitterness, often mixed with exhaustion.

Projectors fear that they will not be invited. However, if you follow your Strategy of waiting for the invitation, what happens is that your aura's frequency starts to change. The more you live according to your design, the more invitations you get. This will bring you SUCCESS. Once invited, you don't need to wait for any more invitations regarding whatever you were invited to (project, job, relationship, et cetera). Just follow your Authority in doing what you do and don't initiate.

The invitation, the correct entry into anything, is the key. The feeling of being recognized, appreciated, heard, and seen. Is it there? Great. If not, you may stop talking in mid-sentence and save yourself yet one more disappointment of not being understood.

Your openness can be energetically exhausting, so it is important to have your own space to relax. The same advice regarding sleeping applies to you as to everyone else with an undefined Sacral: go to bed as soon as you begin to feel tired and if possible, sleep alone (see Manifestors for details).

While the natural role (and instinct) of the Projector is to "manage, guide and direct others," the Projector can only do so effectively when others want to be managed, guided, and directed! Projectors are the eternal students of humanity and system masters. You need to have a system through which you can relate and understand life.

As mentioned at the beginning, most people don't like to be given advice or told what to do if they haven't first asked for that advice or guidance. Projectors who are not using their energy—and their inherent wisdom—correctly are often perceived as:

- Pushy.
- Bossy.
- Nosy.
- Annoying or irritating.
- Bitter.
- Ignored and literally not heard when they speak.

Projectors who use their energy CORRECTLY are respected and sought-after for their knowledge, talent, and guidance.

Emotional Theme

The BEST approach for a Projector is to wait to be asked or invited before sharing their advice, opinion, feedback, guidance, or direction. When someone asks, that is an indication that he or she wants the guidance and inherent wisdom of that Projector. (Even if that person is completely unaware that they are asking a Projector, that person is unconsciously reacting to the Projector's energetic configuration). That person will then hear and appreciate the value of the Projector's input because they were open to receiving it.

The NEXT BEST approach for the Projector is to at least wait for some recognition and an opening in which to speak. Make eye contact and wait to sense an opportunity to speak without barging into a conversation or seeming pushy or overbearing. When using this NEXT BEST approach, the most effective way for a Projector to begin is to say something like:

> *I have some experience that may be helpful to you, would it be all right if I share it with you?*
>
> *I have some insights about that, may I tell you about them?*
>
> *Perhaps I could be of help, would you mind if I try?*

You still may not get the response that is a clear invitation, but this at least gives the Projector a tiny opening to moving their powerful wisdom out into the world.

Relationships

Projectors in relationships need recognition and attention. It all starts at the very beginning of the relationship. Correct relationships for Projectors have to start with an invitation. Projectors need to be invited into a relationship to make the energy flow work. Once a Projector is invited into a relationship, they can simply enjoy being in the relationship. The right initiating energy sets the tone for the relationship.

If you're a Projector in love, you need to be with your partner, but you also need alone time to maintain and sustain your energy. You may even find that you feel better when you sleep alone in your own aura. Because, as a Projector, you experience sexual energy from outside of yourself and often in a variable way, you may find that it feels like your partner controls or limits that aspect of your relationship. Conversely, you may also find that sometimes you simply don't have the energy for sex or intimacy. This is probably not personal or a function of the relationship, just simply a sign that you need some alone time for regeneration and renewal.

If you love a Projector, when you are the recipient of a Projector's incorrect use of their energy and wisdom, it is easy to feel irritated, turned off, and even repelled. This is normal. Even Projectors can feel turned off and repelled by other Projectors! However, you will miss the wisdom and advice that may very well benefit you. Now that you understand a little about Projectors, the best thing YOU can do is:

- Recognize that their intention is to be helpful.
- Recognize that they are inherently wise and usually have valuable input.
- Recognize that they are simply not using their energy correctly.
- Don't take it personally.
- If you're so inclined, give them attention and energy.
- Invite them to share their ideas with you.

- If you just want to get away from them, get out of their aura for a while and then ask for their opinion or guidance the next time you see them—before they offer it.

Projectors have a life purpose of managing and guiding others in their process of creation. Projectors are inherently intuitive and wise about others. A Projector can watch Manifestors, Generators, and Manifesting Generators and instantly be conscious of what needs to happen to make their impact more effective and easier. This is a natural and intricate part of the Projector personality. If you watch young children Projectors, they manage their parents and their peers with great awareness as well as clarity. This can often earn them the reputation of being "bossy," controlling, or a "know it all."

The reason this inherent wisdom is constantly misunderstood is because collectively we don't know how to make the most of the energy of the Projectors.

Projector Children

Projector children need to show their value over and over and over again. The greatest gift you can give your Projector is a sense of their own inner wisdom and value. Projector children need to be taught to wait for recognition. The child also needs to learn to trust that when her she is quiet and waiting for the right people who truly value who they are, the Projector can then freely share what it is they know and have to offer.

Projector children need invitations and, as a parent, you may need to facilitate invitations for them. You may even need to help them find jobs and opportunities for your teens because it can be very challenging (and incorrect) for Projectors to go out and find work.

Projectors don't have the same quality of energy as other Types. That means it isn't always easy for them to do chores that require lots of physical work, like mowing the yard. Find chores that suit the Projector nature. Your Projector children will thrive if you give them the opportunity to organize and manage your family.

Your Projector child may find that "regular" life is taxing and exhausting. You might need to slow down your life and find ways for your Projector to replenish their energy on a weekly basis. For instance, it's not healthy for the Projector child to be deeply committed to lots of after-school activities. Sports and physical activities may be limited for the Projector, and they may tire more easily than other children.

Work

The Projector Strategy is to wait to be invited into the big opportunities in life. These big invitations come infrequently, every two to three years. Big opportunities are things like love, marriage, moving, getting a new job, etc. In between the big invitations, Projectors don't have to wait for small things such as going to a movie or going out to eat. Projectors don't need to wait for anything except *big invitations;* waiting for those is an important part of helping the Projector find the place in life where they are valued and loved for who they really are.

Projectors are not here to manage and guide everyone. They have their own group of people or "tribe" who waits to be managed by them. To find their "people," Projectors have to be recognized or invited into sharing their wisdom.

In a society where we are taught to go out and make life happen, waiting for recognition and invitations from others can feel like a painful and agonizingly slow process. Because Projectors are often trained to act differently than their true nature, they can get very busy pushing people to see and recognize them. They often miss the true invitations that come their way because they're too busy doing what they've been trained that they "need" to or "should" by others.

Health

Pushing and forcing will never have a positive outcome for Projectors. In fact, pushing and forcing will always have the opposite effect and lead to burnout. The more a Projector attempts to push, force, or struggle their way into being "seen" or recognized, the more invisible they become.

Not only that, Projectors have a very finite amount of energy, and are not meant to work in the traditional way work is designed. If pushed into situations that don't recognize inherent, intuitive gifts, or involves hard physical labor, Projectors will burnout.

Projectors can't make life work for them if they follow the standard definitions of what it takes to be successful in life, although Projectors can be powerful and very successful. (For example, President Obama and President Kennedy are both Projectors.)

When Projectors push or force, they push people away rather than attracting them. Because working hard isn't really an option for the limited energy of the Projector, no matter how hard they try, the Projector can often feel that life isn't "fair" and become bitter.

Projectors must go to bed and relax before they're tired. The nature of how energy works requires the discharge of energy that was stored through the day.

In addition, because very few Projectors are taught how to properly access energy, of all the groups, they can often be the most challenged when it comes to abundance.

Wealth

There are two key factors in creating abundance for the Projector. First of all, the most important thing that a Projector has to master is their own sense of worth and value. A Projector has to wait to be recognized by the right people, the people who value and see them for the gifts they bear. If a Projector is not sitting and waiting for the right people because they question their own value, it makes them bitter, and ultimately causes them to "waste" their wisdom and energy on people who don't value who they are.

Projectors who value themselves enough to wait for the right people to give them invitations are powerfully compelling and frequently turn invitations away. A Projector who values themselves is an abundance magnet.

Secondly, when a Projector learns to trust the abundant trajectory of the Universe and can wait comfortably for the right invitation to arrive, they conserve their precious energy and feel vibrant, vital, and ready for the invitations when they manifest. Burned out Projectors, on the other hand, sometimes turn down good invitations if they've wasted their energy pursuing what's not right for them.

When a Projector is living their wealth theme, they are serving as "midwives" to the world. They guide, coach, and nurture others into fulfilling their roles as initiators and builders. Projectors truly tend to the template of the evolution of the world in every aspect. When Projectors are serving in this capacity, they are strong and powerful blessings to the world around them. They are then magnets for abundant opportunities.

When Projectors first learn their Strategy of waiting for invitations, they often have to dramatically align their current life. Sometimes Projectors have to maintain their "day job" because they need the money. It can be tricky to keep the traditional flow of income and to simultaneously shift to waiting for the right thing to arrive.

It is important for Projectors to do whatever they can do to stay out of the bitterness (the emotional theme of the Projector). While they're waiting, Projectors need to stay in their joy and follow their bliss. It's not unusual for Projectors to take a deep dive into what brings them joy only to find that their next invitation is deeply aligned with the joy they've been pursuing!

Projectors are gifted at knowing others, not so good at knowing themselves. Sometimes Projectors will benefit from having a good friend with whom they can talk not because they need advice, but because they have to see their decisions in the context of someone else for them to know what is right for them. Talking helps a Projector "see" themselves and can be crucial to help them get clarity before making a big decision.

Self-care, rest, restoration, and working on self-worth and value are the most important things Projectors can do to activate their abundance blueprint. When Projectors feel energized and valuable, they transform, not only their loved ones and themselves, but ultimately the world around them. The truth is that Projectors need more attention and energy from other people than any of the other Types.

Spiritual Theme

Projectors truly serve as the "midwives" of the future. They have a deep inner sense of what's possible for the world and know how to direct the necessary energy to bring the non-tangible into form.

They are energy wizards and are, on an unconscious level, constantly realigning and managing the energy flow of the world. This work goes way beyond the tangible physical work of the Generator and Manifestor Types. This is energy, and the Projector keeps the energy grid of creation in place.

Projectors often report being "tired all the time" even when they do "nothing." A Projector is never doing "nothing." They are in a constant state of holding together the energy grid of the world. Because Projectors know energy so well, they are often involved in energy healing and service-based professions. They are natural healers and helpers.

Many Projectors are magnetic, charismatic recipients of amazing invitations. Ringo Starr is a Projector. He was literally "invited" to join The Beatles after one of the original band members left the band. Other famous Projectors include Barak Obama, Nelson Mandela, Queen Elizabeth II, Mick Jagger, Osho, Woody Allen, Barbara Streisand, Liz Taylor, Lance Armstrong, Abraham Lincoln, Leonardo da Vinci, Fidel Castro, Shirley MacLaine, James Joyce, Brad Pitt, John F. Kennedy, Hugh Hefner, Karl Marx, and Marilyn Monroe, Taylor Swift, Kanye West, Chris Brown.

THE DETAILS OF DESIGN

PROJECTOR

AT A GLANCE

Wait for Recognition

Focus:

Guidance
Wisdom • Intuitive
Sensitive • Sharing

Supportive Actions:

♥ Value yourself and your wisdom

♥ Wait for the people who understand you

♥ Rest frequently

♥ Not 9 - 5

♥ Passive revenue

♥ Alone time

♥ Lie down and rest before sleep

Challenges:

💣 Not recognizing burnout

💣 Not knowing when enough is enough

💣 Allowing the support

THE REFLECTOR

FOCUS

Mirror, Community, Right Place,
Timing, Sensitivity

LIFE PURPOSE:

Measure the energy in the community

STRATEGY:

Wait before making decisions, pay attention (wait 28 days)

EMOTIONAL THEME:

Disappointment

WEALTH THEME:

Takes time to make choices

CHALLENGES:

Trusting that certainty, truth, and solution are more
important than anything else.

PERCENTAGE:

Less than 1% Reflectors

ROLE:

Reflecting the health and alignment
of the people around them.

Reflectors are a minority—around 1% of the population are Reflector types. Reflectors have all Centers "open" and their chart looks almost "empty."

Reflectors are fully open to the world and to others. Because there are no defined centers by design, Reflectors take in the energy of everybody else, seeing the world through others eyes, sampling a frequency of energy and reflecting it back to the other.

Reflectors are like a mirror, and the reflection of other people continually change their perception. One instant you may feel extremely emotional while the next moment it's gone. You may then get all the ideas and a sound sense of knowing where you're going in life, and then it's gone again, and so forth. That's why it's very essential for you carefully choose your friends and partners; they will have a huge impact on your feelings and experience of *yourself*.

Reflectors have considerably different life experiences that all of the other Types. So, sometimes they may feel alone and misunderstood. Reflectors can also suffer deep disappointment when having to wait and live through the energy of others.

This type of emotion causes Reflectors to require more attention than most all other people (and Types). Because of this, at times they may feel inadequate and think that they don't *fit* anywhere.

The most uncomfortable thing for Reflectors is pressure, especially the pressure to make decisions. For them, it's the most unnatural thing, because Reflectors don't necessarily make decisions. They experience a choice or decision over a cycle of the Moon (29 days). It's not the same as making a decision with the mind. Reflectors have to experience their choice inside of themselves over time. Going through the entire cycle gives them the power to be able to realize solutions and right choices.

Common Traps and Challenges

Reflectors, with their openness and taking in other people's definition, must wait 29 days before making any major decisions - no matter how certain they feel about something in the moment.

For Reflectors, you have to be in the right geographical location, the place that feels good and like "home" for your life to feel "right." When you are in the right place, you meet the right people, are part of the right community, and your life feels aligned. Under these circumstances, making decisions can feel easier and less disappointing.

Total openness may make you, at times almost *invisible* to others. Not knowing the mechanics of your design, you, Reflector may feel deeply disappointed in life. But that very openness grants the potential for a great wisdom and insight into the potential for humanity (and yourself) if you learn how to work with it correctly.

157

Reflectors often struggle with "merging" in their personal relationships if they don't understand the nature of their openness and their capacity for deep empathy. Sometimes the life of a Reflector can get "hijacked" by the energy of the people surrounding them, and they can lose their own direction in life.

Consistency is vital for the Reflector. Reflectors need to have people whose aura they know. It is common for Reflectors to have lifelong friends and to even have trouble disentangling themselves from the energy of their parents (their family of origin) simply because Reflectors experience so much inconsistently. The consistency of the people they know makes them feel safe.

Reflectors, because of the length of time it takes for them to have clarity, don't transition quickly and need time to make major life changes such as leaving home, moving, starting a new job, even getting married.

Strategy

What Reflectors must know and logically understand is that any kind of pressure they experienced is detrimental to their health. By *taking the time* to make important decisions and knowing that the time spent on considering their resolves is how their success is completed, they will realize how vital it is to keep from letting anyone pressure them.

Reflectors are lunar beings, tied to the lunar cycle, so their Strategy (and sometimes the challenge) is to wait 29 days before making any major decisions. During the 29 days, Reflectors should talk with different people about decisions. As a Reflector, you need to have people in your life who will serve as your sounding board, not because you need advice (you don't), but because you need to hear yourself talk about what you are feeling about your choices.

Life for you is an objective experience. As you move through life, discovering the truth of "this isn't me" over and over again, your openness may be energetically exhausting so it is important to have your own space where you can relax. The same goes concerning rest and sleep. The Reflector has an undefined Sacral; go to bed as soon as you begin to feel tired and if possible, sleep alone.

When centers are open, it doesn't mean they are broken or empty. Your mind can easily judge your characteristics as something bad or wrong, but Reflectors carry in their being a deep potential to know the possibilities for humanity. This can be a beautiful thing.

Emotional Theme

Reflectors have the capacity to sense, feel, and know the full potential of the people and the communities around them. Their Open-ness gives them deep awareness and wisdom about what is possible for the world. It is disappointing for the Reflector to know what's possible and see that the world isn't fulfilling its full potential. Disappointment also comes because the speed of the world and the Reflector's need for ample time to make clear and good decisions don't always match.

When a Reflector fails to take their time in deciding and struggles to find their own energy in the midst of the energy that they are experiencing from others, it's easy for a Reflector to feel pressured into making a choice quickly. (And, of course, collectively we have little patience for people who need time for clarity.)

Consequently, Reflectors can leap into decisions too quickly and then feel disappointed with the long-term consequences of their decisions.

Because of a Reflector's deep capacity to know and connect with the people they love, they prefer to surround themselves with people they've been with for a long time. Many Reflectors also prefer the company of children because the purity of their energy is comforting to Reflectors, who are often disappointed by humanity.

Relationships

Reflectors need people because they are non-energy beings and depend on the energetic connections that others provide them. But, they also need their alone time so that they may discharge energy that they've absorbed through the nine Open Centers.

There are certain things to remember if you are in a relationship with a Reflector as they discharge others' energy that is in their system.

- Love them as they are; don't try to change them, and appreciate their very important role for humanity.
- Reflectors need space, give them the space and time to be themselves.
- Allow them to manage their energy; don't pressure or push them.
- Honor their long decision-making sequences.
- Let them speak as Reflectors need to hear their issues and feelings reflected back to them through you.
- Help them recognize when the environment is not healthy for them.
- Understand that they may need you more than you need them.
- Know that you will see the truth about yourself through them, be okay with that revelation.
- Don't take their disappointments personally; it's their nature, their emotion.

Reflectors can easily "merge" with the people around them. In relationships, they can easily "match" their partners. It is easy for Reflectors to not realize that they are giving up their own needs and wants because they have lost their energetic connection to themselves and their own needs.

Reflector Children

Reflector children present a unique set of challenges for parents. Raising a Reflector requires patience, love, and an awareness that your Reflector child may need more attention and energy that your other children.

The first thing Reflector children need is consistency. Because so much of the Reflector experience is variable, the consistency of the auras of friends, loved ones, and caregivers is vital. They need to know who they can trust, who will be steady and unchanging in the changing energy experience of the Reflector.

This need for consistency can make the Reflector child appear to be "clingy" or "needy." Reflector children need consistent caregivers and very few major life changes, especially at the beginning of their lives.

Transitions and change can be very hard for the Reflector child; they need more time than most children to adjust to change. Cataclysmic changes (for instance, divorce) can leave a Reflector child reeling for a long time. Managing change is easier for the Reflector child if you are patient and understanding. Also, do your best to establish a new foundation in their lives as quickly as possible.

If you are a person who struggles with consistency and routine, it may deeply impact your Reflector child. Setting routines and sticking to them helps the Reflector child feel safe and stable.

Reflector children are deeply emotionally sensitive and can often react to major events that happen on the planet. One Reflector child I know who lived in Boston had a very emotional breakdown a day before the Boston Marathon bombing and was inconsolable for more than a week. Sometimes Reflector children benefit from getting energy work by skilled practitioners to help the release the energy that they hold in their bodies.

Reflector children need to feel good in their space. They need their own room and where they live needs to feel right for them. Reflector children, once they are seven or older (when the aura is mature), fare better sleeping in their own room, away from others. This gives their energy field time to decompress and release the energy of others.

Because Reflectors have an open Sacral Center, some Reflector children will struggle with hard physical chores. The best way to help a Reflector get things done is to do it with them. This can sometimes even be true for homework and other activities.

Finally, Reflector children talk a lot and need to talk to know what they're thinking and feeling. As a parent of a Reflector, you need to allow your child the freedom to dump out their thoughts and resist the urge to give them advice or guidance unless they ask you. They're not asking for guidance. They are simply talking to get clarity. If you give them guidance without being asked, it will trigger their own tendency towards feeling inadequate, or they will feel controlled.

Work

Like the Projector and Manifestor types, Reflectors do not have "sustainable energy." Only Generators and Manifesting Generators have that type of energy. So, with Reflectors, they are not wired to "work" a typical job *sustainably*, which may be an issue in relationships and in earning a living.

While Reflectors can amplify a lot of power and seemingly have a lot of intense energy, they cannot sustain that energy over time. They need cycles of rest and renewal like all open Sacral Types.

Their need to talk and their need to take time to make good choices can sometimes cause them pain in the workplace. Once they are recognized for their empathy and the awareness they bring to the workplace, they can assume their right role of reflecting the health of the business and serve as the powerful barometers that they are.

Reflectors in the workplace can be visionaries and can express the potential of the business as they carry the awareness of what's possible in their energy field.

Health

There are three main factors to staying healthy if you are a Reflector.

You need to be in an environment that feels good to you, and the people in your environment need to be healthy. Because you are so sensitive to others and the experience of others, if you are in an environment where people aren't making healthy choices, that will deeply impact you.

You need good sleep and rest. Like all non-Sacral Types, Reflectors sleep best alone and need to be in the energy of their own aura at night to stay vital and to replenish their energy. Reflectors need to be in bed before they are tired and rest in a prone position until they fall asleep.

You need to take your time to make the decisions that are right for you. If you feel pressured to decide before you're ready, it may end up being the wrong choice and the pressure and struggle to try to feel "right" about the decision can deeply impact your physical and emotional health.

Wealth

Much like with health, so much of the Reflector experience with wealth depends on the environment in which they surround themselves. Your ability to create wealth and be in the flow of abundance will be influenced deeply by the people with whom you associate and where you live your life. You need to be in an environment that offers you the wealth of abundant energy.

A Reflector can make more money and create a strong financial foundation when they take their time to make good choices. Fast-paced money-making strategies don't always play out well for the Reflector because they need time to make good choices. Take your time and invest in opportunities that afford you the time to wait to be clear before you must invest.

Because Reflectors are non-Sacral beings, meaning they need to consciously save and create a financial cushion for themselves to support them when they need a cycle of rest in their life. Starting young with a powerful saving strategy benefits the Reflector the most.

Spiritual Theme

Reflectors are here to be our Karmic Mirrors. Their life experience and their reflection to us reveals where we are in our evolutionary process. The Reflectors in our lives show us how close we are to fulfilling our potential and let us know the emotional maturity and alignment we are experiencing by living it and demonstrating it in their own reflected experience.

The heart of the Reflector carries within it the potential for our optimal evolution and the story of what else is possible for humanity.

Famous Reflectors include Michael Jackson, Sandra Bullock, Uri Geller and Roslyn Carter.

THE DETAILS OF DESIGN

REFLECTOR

AT A GLANCE

Karmic Mirror

Focus:

Mirror • Community
Right Place • Timing
Sensitivity

Supportive Actions:

- ♥ Take your time
- ♥ Surround yourself with people who feel good
- ♥ Know your monthly energy cycle
- ♥ Be conscious of the energy around you
- ♥ Don't take anything personally
- ♥ Beware of merging with others
- ♥ Recognize the inner beauty in others

Challenges:

- ☀ Falling in love with people's potential
- ☀ Energy overwhelm
- ☀ Pressure to make decisions quickly

PUTTING IT ALL TOGETHER AND KEEPING IT SIMPLE

In this section of the Activation Guide, you will need your Human Design chart. Take some time to look at the chart and use these questions to help you discover more about your unique blueprint. Capture your responses to the exercises in your journal.

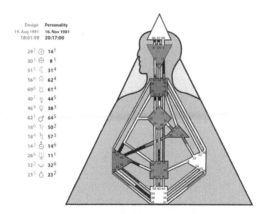

Overview

Type: Generator
    Conditioning Theme: Frustration
    Strategy: Wait to Respond

Profile: 1/3, Investigating Martyr
    14-8 / 29-30: The right angle cross of Contagion(4)
    Right angle - Personal Destiny

Definition: Triple Split Definition

Inner Authority: Sacral Expressed Generated

TYPE

Your Type is the most important information in your chart. When you know your Type you understand more about your purpose, how you best make decisions and some of the challenges facing you as you begin to create a life that is more in alignment with Who You Truly Are.

What is Your Type?

(See page 66 for more information about the Type)

Are you experiencing any of the challenges for your Type?

If so, what can you do to embrace more of the gifts and purpose of your Type?

EMOTIONAL THEME

The Emotional Theme for each Type is part of how the energy moves for your Type. If you understand your Emotional Theme, then you can better stay in the flow of your unique energy and stop feeling as if you're doing something "wrong." The Emotional Theme for each Type is a barometer of how your energy is flowing and will often tell you if you are living in alignment with your energy blueprint.

What is Your Emotional Theme?

(See page 67 for more information about the Emotional Theme)

How has your Emotional Theme impacted your life, your relationships, and your perception of yourself?

STRATEGY

Each Type has a specific way of finding direction in life and making decisions. If you simply know your Type and follow the Strategy for your Type, you will immediately begin to synchronize your life with your Life Purpose, your Soul Purpose, and what you came here to do.

What is Your Strategy?

(See page 68 for more information about the Strategy)

How closely aligned are you with your Strategy?

Are you making decisions correctly for your Type and Strategy?

PROFILE

Your Profile tells you a little more about how you learn, your character, and what you need to feel comfortable in life. You have two lines in your Profile. Both of these line energies need to be honored and fulfilled for you to feel good in life.

What is Your Profile?

What are the two lines in your Profile?

First Line:

Second Line:

(See page 69 for more information about the Profile)

What does your Profile say about you?

How can you allow for more of what your Profile needs to feel comfortable in your life?

DEFINITION

Your Definition is important because it tells you whether your energy is unified and synchronized or if your energy has different aspects that you can access in various situations and in all kinds of relationships.

What is Your Definition?

(See page 75 for more information about the Definition)

How does understanding your definition help you understand yourself better?

What parts of yourself are you now more willing to accept and allow without judgment?

AUTHORITY

Your Authority influences your Strategy.
It doesn't change your Strategy; it just
influences how you live your Strategy.
There are only three Authority
components that really impact how you
live your Strategy: Emotional, Self-
Projected, and Splenic Authority.

What is Your Authority?

(See page 77 for more information about the Authority)

How will you use your Authority to deepen your ability to
make better decisions and live more in alignment with your
Authentic Self?

THE CENTERS

There are nine Centers in the Human Design chart. Each Center is responsible for processing specific kinds of energies:

The Centers

Head Center
Inspiration

Ajna Center
Information and Beliefs

Throat Center
Communication and Manifesting

G-Center
Love and Direction

Will Center
Self-Worth and Value

Sacral Center
Workforce and Life Force Energy

Emotional Solar Plexus
Emotional Energy and Intuition

Spleen Center
Instinct, Timing, and Immune System

Root Center
Adrenaline Energy

WHAT CENTERS DO YOU HAVE DEFINED?

Centers are "defined" when they are "colored." That means that these are energies that you carry and experience consistently and are a part of what you transmit out into the world.

WHAT CENTERS DO YOU HAVE OPEN?

"Open" Centers are white on your Human Design chart. Wherever you have openness in your chart is where you take energy in from others. You don't just take it in, you amplify it, thus making your experience of these energies intense and powerful.

Because you experience openness from outside of yourself, your experience of these energies is inconsistent, variable, and you may often mistakenly think these energies belong to you instead of to others. The more openness you have in your chart, the more sensitive you are and the more potential you must become wise about the potential of the human experience.

Open Centers create predictable behavioral themes. These themes sometimes cause us to engage in self-defeating patterns and habits that hold you back from accessing the wisdom that your openness brings you. These themes also cause us to act out in the world in ways that are not in alignment with your True Self.

MY CENTERS

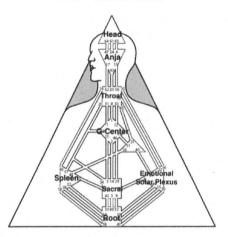

DEFINED	OPEN
_____	_____
_____	_____
_____	_____
_____	_____
_____	_____
_____	_____
_____	_____
_____	_____
_____	_____
_____	_____

Using your chart, list your defined and open Centers
here. Color your defined Centers, if you like.

AFFIRMATIONS FOR MY CENTERS

Use the following affirmations to help you understand the true nature of your energy.

Affirmation for My Defined Head Center

I am inspired and inspiring. I spread inspiration everywhere I go, and I share my ideas as well as inspirations with others.

Affirmation for My Open Head Center

I am deeply inspired all the time. I am wise about what is truly inspiring. I follow my Strategy to help me decide what I need to do. The questions in my head are from others. I don't have to answer all of them. Only the ones that truly excite me!

Affirmations for My Defined Ajna Center

I am gentle with my thinking and always remember that there are many ways to think about information. I am uniquely capable of being certain. I listen carefully to the thoughts of others and allow for limitless thinking with grace.

Affirmation for My Open Ajna Center

I am wise about information and beliefs. My gift is that I can see many sides of an issue and have many different understandings that are fluid and that change all the time. I don't have to make up my mind. I always write down the things I want to remember.

Affirmations for My Defined Throat Center

I speak with great responsibility and know the true source of my words. I allow others to have a voice and I use my words to invite others to share.

Affirmation for My Open Throat Center

My words are heard best when I am invited to speak. I save my words for people who truly desire to hear my point of view and insights. I wait for the right people to ask me and value my words.

Affirmation for My Defined Identity Center

I am who I am. I express myself in all that I do. I celebrate the magnificence of who I am.

Affirmation for My Open Identity Center

How I experience myself changes depending on those around me. I choose to surround myself with people who feel good to me. Place is very important to me, and I create an environment that soothes me. When I am in the right place, the right opportunities come to me.

Affirmation for My Defined Will Center

It is important for me to rest. Rest allows me to recharge my willpower. I honor the promises that I make. I make deliberate promises and understand that people expect me to keep my promises. I am gentle with my expectations of others. Not everyone can just do the things that I do.

Affirmation for My Open Will Center

I enter into all agreements according to my Human Design Strategy. I make promises as well as commitments very carefully and deliberately, and only according to my Human Design Strategy. I have nothing to prove, and I value myself deeply. I fearlessly ask to be paid what I am worth.

Affirmation for My Defined Solar Plexus Center

I take my time making decisions and know that I reach clarity over time. I am here to be deliberate, not spontaneous.

Affirmation for My Open Solar Plexus Center

I can make decisions in the moment. I pay attention to the source of my emotions and allow others to experience their feelings without making their experience my own. I am very sensitive, and I trust my insights about other people's feelings. I take frequent breaks when the emotional energy is too intense.

Affirmation for My Defined Root Center

I honor my root pulse and wait for the energy to get things done. I get more done when the energy is "on." When the energy is off, I know that it is my time to rest and restore myself.

Affirmation for My Open Root Center

I set realistic goals. I make powerful decisions about being free and know that things will get done when they get done. I use pressure to create more energy, and at the end of the day, I rest and relax even if my "to-do" list is long. I make decisions according to my Human Design strategy even if I feel pressure. I breathe and relax knowing there is an abundance of time to get things done.

Affirmation for My Defined Spleen Center

I trust my intuition. I listen to my "gut" feelings and take guided action. I listen to my body. I rest and take care of myself. I honor my sense of time. I remember that not everyone is as fast as me and I flow with Universal Timing.

Affirmation for My Open Spleen Center

I easily let go of all things that do not serve my highest good. I honor my body and the messages it sends me. When I feel sick, I rest. I honor my own sense of timing and know that whenever I arrive is just perfect! I respect other people's sense of time and always wear a watch. I trust my intuition and know that I receive intuitive insights in many ways.

Affirmation for My Defined Sacral Center

I wait with grace and patience knowing that the right opportunities will show up for me. All I have to do is respond to the world, and I will joyfully do the right work and be with the right people. I fearlessly honor my response and know that I am internally driven to be in the right place at the right time, doing the right work.

Affirmation for My Open Sacral Center

I am not here to work in the traditional way. I can work hard in short bursts and then I need alone time to discharge the extra energy I carry. I recognize that my energy is mutable, and I take care of myself and let go of the expectations of others. I am very powerful when I am using my energy correctly.

QUESTIONS FOR MY OPEN CENTERS

Listed below are inquiry questions to help you discover patterns that your openness may be creating in your life. Take some time to answer these questions, capturing your responses in your journal

Head Center
"Am I under pressure to answer other people's questions and live out their ideas and inspirations?"

Ajna Center
"Am I struggling to be certain about making up my mind or to convince others (and myself) that I am certain?"

Throat Center
"Am I trying to get attention (perhaps inappropriately) so that I can be heard?"

Identity (also called "G") Center

"Do I question my lovability? Am I struggling to find direction? Do I love where I live, where I work, and who I'm with?"

Will Center

"What am I trying to prove?"

Emotional Solar Plexus Center

"Am I avoiding truth and conflict, and trying to keep everyone happy?"

Root Center

"Am I still trying to get things done so I can be free?"

Spleen Center

"Am I holding on to things (or people or pain, etc.) for longer than I should?"

Sacral Center

"Do I know when enough is enough?"

CONCLUSION

You are a once in a lifetime event. There has never been, nor will there ever be another person in this Universe like you.

You enter this life with a Soul Plan and a Life Purpose. The unique expression of who you are has a specific reason for being here on the planet right now. You may not always "know" that reason but your life, if you live it authentically, will reveal that purpose to you step by step.

When we are born, the energy of the world begins to take us away from the Truth of Who We Really Are. Your genetic lineage, your experiences, your pain, trauma, and beliefs that you learn from the people around you, condition you away from that Truth.

The Universe is infinitely wise and kind. Despite how we might struggle and even turn away from the Truth of Who We Really Are, the Universe continues to leave us clues all along the way.

Living true to your Human Design Type allows you to interface and connect with the natural abundance of the Cosmic Plan and supports you in aligning with your destiny - the lessons you sought to master before you even incarnated.

It seems counterintuitive sometimes that living true to ourselves simply means following what feels right and good in a way that feels right and good. We do have to struggle to grow at times. Struggle is in our hard-wiring.

Suffering is not.

We suffer when we turn away from ourselves. We suffer when we resist Who We Truly Are. In my 28 years of experience coaching people, resistance to our Authentic Self is the greatest source of pain in people's lives.

You owe it to yourself to live in a way that is true to Who You Really Are.

You also owe it to the world.

Imagine for a moment that every human being on the planet represents a colorful thread that, when woven together, makes a beautiful tapestry. The tapestry is only as beautiful as the sum total of the all the threads. If a thread is out of place, missing or pulled, it affects the entire face of the tapestry.

You play an important part in this world. You are so important that we would not be who we are right now without you.

At this crucial junction in time, the world needs you to take your right place - the place you intended for yourself to take before you even incarnated.

Living true to your Human Design Type and Strategy, allows you to follow the path you set out for yourself, minimize pain and resistance and, ultimately, step into the full and easy expression of Who You Truly Are.

I hope this book has given you some new insights and ideas into how precious and powerful you are. I hope it has helped you remember that you are here for a reason and that the world needs you to be the full expression of your Authentic Self!

Thank you for being YOU!

From my Heart to Yours,

ABOUT THE AUTHOR

Karen Curry Parker is an entrepreneur, teacher, mentor, coach, and #1 best-selling author. She is deeply dedicated to sharing and co-creating a sustainable, abundant global community.

Karen is also the author of ***Understanding Human Design the New Science of Astrology: Discover Who You Really Are, Abundance by Design, The Prosperity Revolution, EFT for Parents,*** and ***Waging Peace*** *in the Face of Rage* and weekly articles about abundance and spirituality. She is the host of the internationally acclaimed podcast, Quantum Conversations.

Karen's website:
www.quantumalignmentsystem.com

Karen is available for private consultations, keynote talks and to conduct in-house seminars and workshops. You can reach her at Karen@quantumalignmentsystem.com.

Made in the USA
Coppell, TX
27 November 2021

66578060R00115